# RUTH

# THE OLD TESTAMENT LIBRARY

Editorial Advisory Board

Kirsten Nielsen

# RUTH
## A Commentary

 Westminster John Knox Press
Louisville, Kentucky

Translated from the Danish by Edward Broadbridge.

*Book design by Jennifer K. Cox*

*First edition*

Published by Westminster John Knox Press
Louisville, Kentucky

This book is printed on acid-free paper that meets the American National Standards Institute Z39.48 standard. ∞

PRINTED IN THE UNITED STATES OF AMERICA

97 98 99 00 01 02 03 04 05 06 — 10 9 8 7 6 5 4 3 2 1

**Library of Congress Cataloging-in-Publication Data**

Nielsen, Kirsten, date.
    Ruth : a commentary / Kirsten Nielsen ; [translated from the Danish by Edward Broadbridge]. — 1st ed.
        p.    cm. — (The Old Testament library)
    Includes bibliographical references and index.
    ISBN 0-664-22092-4 (alk. paper)
    1. Bible. O.T. Ruth—Commentaries.   I. Title.   II. Series.
BS1315.3.N54   1997
222′.35077—dc20                                          96-41719

# CONTENTS

## RUTH

# PREFACE

This commentary on the book of Ruth derives from my interest in Old Testament literature and theology. I have therefore read Ruth as a part of the Old Testament canon and emphasized the book's close relation to other women's narratives in the Old Testament. By placing Ruth in its intertextuality I seek to show the background against which the audience and readers of the time would have understood the book, as well as the social and political situations within which Ruth has functioned as a defense of the claims of David's family to the kingship. For a work of literature such as Ruth is not only great art but also a piece of *Realpolitik*. This version of the story of God's election of a family ancestress presents the convincing argument that it was through a foreign woman, the Moabite Ruth, that God chose David and his family to sit on the throne of Israel.

The book was written in Aarhus, Denmark, and at Emory University in Atlanta, U.S.A. I am very grateful to the students who have taken part in my classes on Ruth for their interest in my work. Special thanks go to Bodil Højberg, who with enthusiasm and erudition has read the manuscript and suggested improvements. During my stay in Atlanta in the early summer of 1994 I received invaluable help from, among others, Robert Detweiler and Pat Graham, while at the same time enjoying the privilege of access to the excellent Pitts Theology Library. I think of my friends there and in Denver with deep gratitude. Finally I wish especially to thank Edward Broadbridge for inspiring cooperation during the translation.

The book is dedicated to my husband, Leif Nielsen, who as always has given me his untiring support and encouragement.

*Aarhus 1996*

# ABBREVIATIONS

| | |
|---|---|
| *AJSL* | *The American Journal of Semitic Languages and Literatures* |
| *ANET* | *Ancient Near Eastern Texts Relating to the Old Testament,* edited by James B. Pritchard, Third Edition with Supplement, Princeton, 1969 |
| *ASTI* | *Annual of the Swedish Theological Institute* |
| *BASOR* | *Bulletin of the American Schools of Oriental Research* |
| *BHS* | *Biblia Hebraica Stuttgartensia* |
| BKAT | Biblischer Kommentar Altes Testament |
| *HTR* | *Harvard Theological Review* |
| *JBL* | *Journal of Biblical Literature* |
| *JJS* | *Journal of Jewish Studies* |
| *JRAS* | *Journal of the Royal Asiatic Society* |
| *JSOT* | *Journal for the Study of the Old Testament* |
| *JSS* | *Journal of Semitic Studies* |
| LXX | Septuagint |
| MT | Masoretic Text |
| *RB* | *Revue Biblique* |
| *SJOT* | *Scandinavian Journal of the Old Testament* |
| *TB* | *Tyndale Bulletin* |
| *TZ* | *Theologische Zeitschrift* |
| *VT* | *Vetus Testamentum* |
| *VT Supp* | *Vetus Testamentum, Supplements* |
| *ZAW* | *Zeitschrift für die alttestamentliche Wissenschaft* |

# SELECT BIBLIOGRAPHY

*I. Commentaries*

Campbell, Edward F., Jr. *Ruth: A New Translation with Introduction, Notes, and Commentary.* Anchor Bible. New York, 1975.

Frevel, Christian. *Das Buch Ruth.* Neuer Stuttgarter Kommentar: Altes Testament, 6. Stuttgart, 1992.

Gerleman, Gillis. *Rut—Das Hohelied.* Biblischer Kommentar Altes Testament 18. Neukirchen-Vluyn, 1965.

Gray, John. *Joshua, Judges and Ruth.* Century Bible. New edition. London, 1967.

Gressmann, Hugo. *Die Anfänge Israels (Von 2. Mose bis Richter und Ruth).* Die Schriften des Alten Testaments 1. Abteilung: *Die Sagen des Alten Testaments.* 2. Band, 263–79. Göttingen, 1922.

Haller, Max. *Die fünf Megilloth.* Handbuch zum Alten Testament 18, 1–20. Tübingen, 1940.

Hertzberg, Hans Wilhelm. *Die Bücher Josua, Richter, Ruth.* Das Alte Testament Deutsch, 9. Göttingen, 1953.

Hubbard, Robert L., Jr. *The Book of Ruth.* New International Commentary on the Old Testament. Grand Rapids, 1988.

Rudolph, Wilhelm. *Das Buch Ruth, Das Hohe Lied, Die Klagelieder.* Kommentar zum Alten Testament. XVII, 1–3. Gütersloh, 1962.

Sasson, Jack M. *Ruth: A New Translation with a Philological Commentary and a Formalist-Folklorist Interpretation.* Baltimore and London, 1979. 2d ed., Sheffield, 1989.

Würthwein, Ernst. *Die fünf Megilloth, Ruth, Das Hohelied, Esther.* 2d revised ed. Handbuch zum Alten Testament, 18. Tübingen, 1969.

Zakovitch, Y. *Ruth: Introduction and Commentary* (Heb.). Tel Aviv and Jerusalem, 1990.

Zenger, Erich. *Das Buch Ruth.* Zürcher Bibelkommentar, Altes Testament. Vol. 8. Zurich, 1986.

## II. Monographs

Beattie, D.R.G. *Jewish Exegesis of the Book of Ruth*. Sheffield, 1977.

Carmichael, Calum M. *Women, Law, and the Genesis Traditions*. Edinburgh, 1979.

Fewell, Danna Nolan, and David Miller Gunn. *Compromising Redemption: Relating Characters in the Book of Ruth*. Literary Currents in Biblical Interpretation. Louisville, Ky., 1990.

Gow, Murray D. *The Book of Ruth: Its Structure, Theme and Purpose*. Leicester, 1992.

Hals, R. M. *The Theology of the Book of Ruth*. Philadelphia, 1969.

Johnson, Marshall D. *The Purpose of the Biblical Genealogies, with Special Reference to the Setting of the Genealogies of Jesus*. Cambridge, 1969.

Leggett, Donald A. *The Levirate and Goel Institutions in the Old Testament, with Special Attention to the Book of Ruth*. Cherry Hill, N.J.: Mack, 1974.

Myers, Jacob M. *The Linguistic and Literary Forms of the Book of Ruth*. Leiden, 1955.

Trible, Phyllis. *God and the Rhetoric of Sexuality*. Philadelphia, 1978.

Wilson, Robert R. *Genealogy and History in the Biblical World*. New Haven, Conn., and London, 1977.

Witzenrath, Hagia Hildegard. *Das Buch Ruth: Eine literaturwissenschaftliche Untersuchung*. Munich, 1975.


## III. Articles

Anderson, A. A. "The Marriage of Ruth," *JSS* 23 (1978): 171–83.

Beattie, D.R.G. "Kethibh and Qere in Ruth IV 5," *VT* 21 (1971): 490–94.

———. "The Book of Ruth as Evidence for Israelite Legal Practice," *VT* 24 (1974): 251–67.

———. "Ruth III," *JSOT* 5 (1978): 39–48.

———. "Redemption in Ruth, and Related Matters: A Response to Jack M. Sasson," *JSOT* 5 (1978): 65–68.

Black, James. "Ruth in the Dark: Folktale, Law and Creative Ambiguity in the Old Testament," *Literature and Theology* 5 (1991): 20–35.

Bos, Johanna W. H. "Out of the Shadows: Genesis 38; Judges 4:17–22; Ruth 3," *Semeia* 42 (1988): 37–67.

Brenner, Athalya. "Naomi and Ruth," *VT* 33 (1983): 385–97.

Burrows, Millar. "Levirate Marriage in Israel," *JBL* 59 (1940): 23–33.

———. "The Marriage of Boaz and Ruth," *JBL* 59 (1940): 445–54.

———. "The Ancient Oriental Background of Hebrew Levirate Marriage," *BASOR* 77 (1940): 2–15.

Campbell, Edward F., Jr. "The Hebrew Short Story: A Study of Ruth," in Howard N. Bream, Ralph D. Heim, and Carey A. Moore, eds., *A Light unto*

*My Path: Old Testament Studies in Honor of Jacob M. Meyers.* Philadelphia, 1974.

Davies, Eryl W. "Inheritance rights and the Hebrew levirate marriage," *VT* 31 (1981): 138–44, 257–68.

———. "Ruth IV 5 and the duties of the *gōʾēl*," *VT* 33 (1983): 231–34.

Fisch, Harold. "Ruth and the structure of covenant history," *VT* 32 (1982): 425–37.

Gordis, Robert. "Love, Marriage, and Business in the Book of Ruth: A Chapter in Hebrew Customary Law." In *A Light unto My Path: Old Testament Studies in Honor of Jacob M. Myers,* edited by Howard N. Bream, Ralph D. Heim, and Carey A. Moore, 241–64. Philadelphia, 1974.

Green, Barbara. "The Plot of the Biblical Story of Ruth," *JSOT* 23 (1982): 55–68.

Gunkel, Hermann. "Ruth." In *Reden und Aufsätze,* 65–92. Göttingen, 1913.

Johnson, A. R. "The Primary Meaning of the Root *gʾl*," *VT Supp* 1 (1953): 67–77.

Kronholm, Tryggve. "The Portrayal of Characters in Midrash Ruth Rabbah: Observations on the formation of the Jewish hermeneutical legend known as 'biblical haggadah'," *ASTI* 12 (1983): 13–54.

Kruger, Paul A. "The Hem of the Garment in Marriage: The Meaning of the Symbolic Gesture in Ruth 3:9 and Ezek. 16:8," *Journal of Northwest Semitic Languages* 12 (1984): 79–86.

Labuschagne, C. J. "The Crux in Ruth 4,11," *ZAW* 79 (1967): 364–67.

Levine, Amy-Jill. "Ruth." In *The Women's Bible Commentary,* edited by Carol A. Newsom and Sharon H. Ringe, 78–84. Louisville, Ky., 1992.

Mettinger, Tryggve N. D. "Intertextuality: Allusion and Vertical Context Systems in Some Job Passages." In *Of Prophets' Visions and the Wisdom of Sages: Essays in Honor of R. Norman Whybray on his Seventieth Birthday,* edited by Heather A. McKay and David J. A. Clines, 257–80. Sheffield, 1993.

Niditch, Susan. "The Wronged Woman Righted: An Analysis of Genesis 38," *HTR* 72 (1979): 143–49.

———. "Legends of Wise Heroes and Heroines: II. Ruth." In *The Hebrew Bible and its Modern Interpreters,* edited by Douglas A. Knight and Gene M. Tucker, 451–56. Philadelphia, 1985.

Nielsen, Kirsten. "Le choix contre le droit dans le livre de Ruth. De l'aire de battage au tribunal," *VT* 35 (1985): 201–12.

Phillips, A. "The Book of Ruth—Deception and Shame," *JJS* 37 (1986): 1–17.

Plum, Karin Friis. "Genealogy as Theology," *SJOT* 1 (1989): 66–92.

Porten, Bezalel. "The Scroll of Ruth: A Rhetorical Study," *Gratz College Annual of Jewish Studies* 7 (1978): 23–49.

Prinsloo, W. S. "The theology of the book of Ruth," *VT* 30 (1980): 330–41.

Rowley, H. H. "The Marriage of Ruth." In *The Servant of the Lord and Other Essays on the Old Testament,* 163–86. London, 1952.

Sasson, Jack M. "Ruth III: A Response," *JSOT* 5 (1978): 49–51.

———. "The Issue of *Ge'ullāh* in Ruth," *JSOT* 5 (1978): 52–64.

Thompson, Thomas and Dorothy. "Some Legal Problems in the Book of Ruth," *VT* 18 (1968): 79–99.

Wilson, Robert R. "The Old Testament Genealogies in Recent Research," *JBL* 94 (1975): 169–89.

# INTRODUCTION

## 1. Contents and Structure

The book of Ruth deals with the Moabite woman Ruth and how it came about that she of all people became the ancestress of Israel's greatest monarch, King David. One of the purposes of the book is therefore to demonstrate that when a foreign woman was given this role it was because God himself had chosen her, just as in his time he had chosen the patriarchs and their family. The story of Ruth is among the best, most charming narratives in the Old Testament—a literary masterpiece. Yet it is also a political statement on behalf of David's dynasty.

The book begins with a famine that forces a man from Bethlehem, Elimelech, to leave Judah together with his wife, Naomi, and their two sons. They seek refuge in Moab, where their sons marry two Moabite women, Ruth and Orpah. Both marriages remain childless, and after some years Elimelech and his sons die, leaving the three women alone. Ruth then chooses to stay with her mother-in-law, Naomi, and returns with her to Judah.

In Bethlehem Ruth meets a relative of her late husband called Boaz, while she is gleaning in his field. Boaz is kind to Ruth, and at Naomi's suggestion Ruth seeks him out later at the threshing floor in the hope that he will marry her, for Boaz is the kinsman-redeemer of Naomi and Ruth. Despite various difficulties Naomi's plan is successful; Ruth and Boaz marry and have a son. The book ends with their genealogy, culminating in David's name.

### The Sequence of Events in Ruth[1]

I.   The husbands die in Moab, and Ruth and Naomi return home to Judah (chap. 1)

[1]Cf. Bezalel Porten, *The Scroll of Ruth*, 1978, 23–49, whose content definition I accept. In the first two chapters, however, I divide up the text slightly differently from Porten, who divides chap. 1 into vv. 1–6, 7–19a, 19b–22, and chap. 2:4–23 into vv. 4–18a and 18b–23. The many rhetorical devices employed by the author of Ruth are analyzed in detail by Porten and Murray D. Gow, and despite differences of approach Gow accepts Porten's definition of the main structure of the book (Murray D. Gow, *The Book of Ruth*, 1992, 92).

    A. After living in Moab ten years, Elimelech and his sons die (1:1–5)

    B. When Naomi wishes to return home, Ruth clings to her, but Orpah leaves (1:6–18)

    C. On arrival in Bethlehem Naomi laments her loss to the townswomen (1:19–22)

II. Ruth gleans in Boaz's field (chap. 2)

    D. Naomi consents to Ruth's plan to glean (2:1–3)

    E. Boaz shows favor to Ruth (2:4–17)

    F. Naomi and Ruth discuss what has happened (2:18–23)

III. Ruth seeks out Boaz at the threshing floor (chap. 3)

    $D_1$. Ruth accepts Naomi's plan that she should go to the threshing floor (3:1–6)

    $E_1$. Boaz again shows favor to Ruth (3:7–15)

    $F_1$. Naomi and Ruth discuss what has happened (3:16–18)

IV. Boaz marries Ruth, who becomes the ancestress of David's line (chap. 4)

    $B_1$. Boaz states publicly that he wishes to marry Ruth, and the anonymous kinsman-redeemer withdraws (4:1–12)

    $C_1$. The women of Bethlehem rejoice at the birth of Naomi's grandchild (4:13–17)

    $A_1$. Ten generations are born in Israel (4:18–22)

### *The Structure of Ruth*

Ruth is one of the best-structured books in the Old Testament. It consists of four chapters, each of which comprises three smaller sections. Out of these twelve parts a unity is created that convinces the reader that the book ends precisely as intended.

A significant characteristic of the book's style is its widespread use of dialogue in which the main characters, though never Naomi and Boaz together, confront one another. Of the 85 verses in the book, no fewer than 55 are in dialogue form. Gathered around these are narrative sections that partly add background to what is to follow (e.g., 1:1–5) and partly create a transition from one section to the next, as, for example, the ending of the first two chapters.

On the basis of these observations a description of the book's structure is best undertaken through a treatment of the individual scenes that constitute the general narrative. Changes of time, place, action, and grouping of persons determine the criteria for this division, and it will become apparent that throughout the book there is a constant movement between Bethlehem and other places: Bethlehem—Moab—Bethlehem—the field—Bethlehem—the threshing floor—Bethlehem—the town gate—Bethlehem. Thus the book ends where it began, in the town linked to the name of David.

Another approach, employed by Murray D. Gow in his comprehensive analysis of the structure of Ruth, is through the rhetorical devices that the author utilizes. In this case there is an emphasis on the frequent use of circle compositions. This is seen at its clearest in the general structuring of the book, which starts with a series of genealogical particulars and ends with a formal genealogy. As outlined in the above sequence of events the book is built on the structure ABC DEF $D_1E_1F_1$ $B_1C_1A_1$, an almost perfect chiastic composition. The first and last chapters correspond to each other, just as the two middle chapters reflect, and must be read in the light of, each other. In his rhetorical-critical analysis Gow demonstrates how chapters 2, 3, and 4 are each built on a similar principle.[2] The author also employs smaller chiasma (cf. the relationship between 1:6ab and 1:7ab, or the mention of Elimelech's relative, Boaz, in 2:1 and 2:3).

Gow's emphasis on the author's preference for chiastic structures is important for an interpretation of the text, since it enables the reader to see where the central statements are to be found. Thus it is not mere coincidence that in both chapters 2 and 3 Boaz's wish that the Lord should bless Ruth forms the fulcrum.

Parallelisms are also frequently employed (e.g., between 1:3ab and 1:5ab, or 1:12 and 1:21). A further common rhetorical device is the repetition of key concepts, such as "return home," "glean," "show favor," "find favor," "lie down," "kinsman-redeemer." We also find retellings of previous events—flashbacks—when Ruth relates her experiences to Naomi at the end of both chapters 2 and 3. The author can also anticipate coming events, such as Naomi's good wishes for her daughters-in-law (1:8–9), and Boaz's wishes for Ruth (2:12), wishes that are fulfilled in the course of the story. In various ways these devices serve to create a coherence between the individual parts and in the book as a unity.

Thus, on account of its dramatic as well as its poetic character, the book can be divided up on the basis of both its narrative action of events and its rhetorical devices, with each approach supplementing the other. In fact they often lead to the same result. On the other hand, it occasionally turns out that where the narrative action appears to have reached a natural break, the author has ensured, perhaps through a chiastic construction, that the reader is not stopped short but is led on. This is the case in the transition from 1:5 to 1:6, where the action moves from a description of life in Moab to Naomi's decision to return home. But at the same time the first five verses form part of a larger chiastic structure comprising 1:1–7b, which contains information on the two Moabite wives as its central element.[3]

Further examples are the transitions from chapters 1 to 2 and 2 to 3, where

---

[2]Gow, *Book of Ruth*, 46, 64, 81–82.
[3]See Gow, *Book of Ruth*, 28–30.

a single statement functions both as a conclusion and as a new beginning, like a hinge holding the separate sections together. Whatever divisions are therefore chosen, they will inevitably involve a break in other contexts, yet it is precisely the contexts across the breaks that confirm the continuity of the narrative. It must be heard or read at one sitting.

By contrast, it is often the sequence of events that leads the reader on, while the chiastic structure creates a roundedness and a feeling of coming to an end. Thus Gow's analysis of chapter 4 demonstrates that the first 11 verses are a chiastic structure, with v. 5 as the fulcrum. At v. 11b[4] the actual legal case that began with the preparations in v. 1 is brought to a conclusion. But there is no major break here, since the result of the legal action has certain consequences which the subsequent blessings express. Nor does the Masoretic Text separate the legal case from the bystanders' wishes for the coming marriage, but allows the two to merge into each other.

Indications of time and tempo also serve the author's purpose in structuring the book. The first chapter opens with a time signal on the lines of "Once upon a time. . . . " All that is known about the sojourn in Moab is that it lasted roughly ten years, and about the return home that it was at the start of the barley harvest. The events of the chapter thus stretch over a fairly long period, not clearly defined. Chapter 2, on the other hand, deals with the relatively brief harvest season (barley and wheat). After this events move rapidly, with chapter 3 covering a single night and chapter 4, a short legal scene, leading swiftly to the desired result: marriage and pregnancy.

Then, however, the tempo decreases markedly and we find the text involved again with a lengthy period of time, as at the beginning of the book. Now we hear about the months of pregnancy, and the family tree is listed generation by generation. Also there is a circular movement in the way time is depicted, with the book ending where it began, in a whole period. Within a few chapters we have moved from the period of Judges to Kings.

Another characteristic of the book's composition is the summarizing and evaluating dialogues that take place in each chapter. At the conclusion of chapter 1 Naomi comments on her own situation to the women of Bethlehem. It is her evaluation that is to form the background for the coming events. The same thing happens in the following chapters, where Naomi comments to Ruth on the day's events in chapter 2 and the night's events in chapter 3, while it is the neighboring wives in chapter 4 who comment to Naomi on the birth of Obed. The choice of this form allows the author time and again to put conclusions into the mouths of women, a factor that is hardly insignificant in a book about the choice of a woman.

---

[4]Gow follows LXX in this verse, with a division between v. 11b, where the legal case ends, and 11c with the blessings for the coming wedding. See Gow, *Book of Ruth*, 1992, 77–81.

The structure of the book of Ruth is marked by efforts to create both a roundedness and a forward drive in the narrative. For example, even though each of the four chapters is well-rounded, the reader is given a clear signal at the conclusion of each chapter as to what the next scene will be about. The structure of the book thus creates a feeling of a conscious control without the reader knowing beforehand how the initial unhappiness will be transformed into a happy conclusion. The fact that the rounded form does not create a closed room is also evident in that the book ends in a genealogy. This list of names rounds off the story but at the same time excites the reader to ask for more stories. What happened to this David who ends the book? The many intertextual signals have the same effect on the reader. The book may have come to an end, but it is clearly part of a much wider network.

Ruth deals with a series of crises which are gradually overcome so that emptiness is transformed into fullness. The famine in Judah is overcome by the journey to Moab. The loss of husbands is redressed in Ruth's case by her marriage to Boaz. And, finally, the lack of an heir is remedied with the birth of Obed, who proves even to be the ancestor of David. We are left in no doubt that behind these events there is a guiding hand that can send famine and elect kings.

## 2.  Genre

Ruth belongs to the narrative genre. Hermann Gunkel has given the classic definition of the book as a *novelle,* a short story, more specifically an idyll.[5] By "idyll" he means to stress the poetic and thus the literary qualities of the short story. Erich Zenger on the other hand points out that "idyll" underplays the action aspect of the book. Not only is a sequence of actions narrated, but behind it stands the real enactor, God himself. It is God's actions we are to learn about, not a series of admirable human qualities. Ruth therefore belongs together with the Joseph narrative and the book of Jonah as regards genre.[6]

It is characteristic of both Gunkel and Zenger to regard the short story as being the narrative, but to exclude the final David genealogy, which they take to be a later addition and therefore of no regard here. Indeed, there has long been general agreement that Ruth 4:18–22 is an addition. Edward F. Campbell calls these verses an editorial appendix,[7] while Ernst Würthwein[8]

---

[5]Hermann Gunkel. "Ruth," in *Reden und Aufsätze,* 1913, 84–86. A meticulous survey of researchers' definitions of the genre of Ruth is to be found in Hagia Hildegard Witzenrath, *Das Buch Ruth,* 1975, 362–68.

[6]See Eric Zenger, *Das Buch Ruth,* 1986, 22–25.

[7]Edward F. Campbell, Jr., *Ruth: A New Translation with Introduction, Notes, and Commentary,* 1975, 170.

[8]Ernst Würthwein, *Die fünf Megilloth,* 1969, 24.

speaks of the secondary nature of the genealogy. Behind these formulations lies the tacit assumption that the narrative existed before the genealogy. However, recent research shows that this assumption is far from being matter of course. Not least, studies of the book's structure and purpose have demonstrated that the genealogy performs an important function in the story's totality.

In his *Anatomy of Criticism*[9] the Canadian literary critic Northrop Frye points out that the purpose of assigning a genre to a text is not so much to classify as to clarify, that is, to uncover the literary ties to which the text is linked. As a result the many definitions of Ruth as a legend, a fairytale, a romance, an idyll, a folktale, or a short story must be seen as an attempt to find the texts alongside which the book can be read and understood. We might even say that the choice of genre is the writer's signal to the reader as to how the text should be read.

Jack M. Sasson, whose commentary includes a number of recent views from the world of folklore, has put forward the thesis that the book is created on the model of a folktale. Ruth is *not* actually a folktale; it is a piece of literature created by educated writers.[10] But it must be read in the same way as we hear a folktale. Here Sasson builds on Vladimir Propp's analyses of a group of Russian folktales, and demonstrates a clear structural similarity between those tales and Ruth. He stresses that a folktale is a closed form with no loose ends left at its conclusion. "Because a folktale leaves nothing that is unresolved, it becomes a self-contained entity. It is unnecessary, therefore, for a folktale to be burdened either by a historical background or by a sequel meant to link it with datable narratives. Thus, unlike other biblical narratives that gain by, indeed depend on, a historical setting, Ruth could easily be lifted out of the period of the Judges and still be appreciated as a superb work of art."[11]

Despite its roundedness Sasson has difficulty with the conclusion of the book, since it is unusual for a folktale to end with a genealogy. In fact Ruth is the only example of this in the Old Testament, according to Sasson.[12] He therefore considers whether the genealogy of 4:18–22 does not rather denote a new beginning to the folktale, or is perhaps the start of a new folktale about Obed: "From a Proppian perspective, *the genealogy of 4:18–22 actually begins the tale of Obed, rather than ends that of Boaz!*"[13]

However, this view stands in some contrast to Sasson's argument earlier in the commentary that the genealogy was tailor-made for the ending of the

---

[9]Northrop Frye, *Anatomy of Criticism*, 1975, 247–48.

[10]Jack M. Sasson, *Ruth: A New Translation with a Philological Commentary and a Formalist-Folklorist Interpretation*, 1989, 214f.

[11]Sasson, *Ruth*, 216.

[12]Sasson, *Ruth*, 179.

[13]Sasson, *Ruth*, 213.

book.[14] Of course he is right that Ruth is the only *clearly* rounded text in the Old Testament that concludes with a genealogy, but in classifying the book as a folktale he forgets that in practice a classification means a clarification, in the sense of a clarity about which other texts the reader should relate to the one in question. What the contemporary reader knew in those days was a series of tales in which genealogies were a matter of course. If we were to assign a genre to Ruth within the Old Testament's own literary forms, the most obvious one would be the patriarchal narratives, which also have many structural similarities precisely with the folktale.

Where Ruth is a single account culminating in a genealogy,[15] the patriarchal narratives are linked into a chain of tales that often end with a genealogy (Gen. 22:20–24; 25:1–4; 25:12–18; 25:19ff.; 35:23–29; 36). Genealogies in patriarchal times round off a story but are simultaneously new beginnings in the accounts of Jacob's sons and their internal rivalries (cf. the expression "Jacob's genealogy," Jacob's *tôlĕdôt,* stands in Gen. 37:2 as the introduction to the Joseph narratives).

In similar fashion the genealogy in Ruth functions as the conclusion to the book while simultaneously pointing forward to new tales, namely of the last shoot on the vine, David. Characteristic for such family histories is that one story gives birth to another, so to speak.[16]

Sasson's difficulty in deciding whether 4:18–22 is the natural ending of the book or the start of a new tale comes about because he settles on the genre of folktale and defines the book accordingly as a clearly delimited work of art that does not point beyond the text itself. For if there is one single characteristic of a genealogy it is that it points beyond the limits of the individual narrative to new generations (or previous generations) and their life stories.

A further difficulty with Sasson's method is his assertion that Ruth should be read independently of time. By sticking to the dogma of the independence and roundedness of the text he prevents himself from questioning beyond the literary work's own limits to its social function (see Introduction, pp. 21–28).

All in all therefore we must conclude that the texts in the Old Testament that Ruth most closely resembles are the patriarchal narratives. In a combination of narrative and genealogy Ruth presents both the particular events that took place when God elected a Moabite woman and the line of descent of which she

---

[14]Sasson, *Ruth,* 180.

[15]In this connection, however, it should be considered whether the placing of Ruth between Judges and 1 Samuel, as is the case in LXX, can be seen as a continuation of the structure that we know from the patriarchal narratives, where the genealogy functions as a link between the individual tales.

[16]Cf. Westermann's formulation in connection with the genealogies in the Yahwist: "Die Genealogien . . . sind geradezu so etwas wie Pflanzstätten von Erzählungen vielerlei Art." Claus Westermann, *Genesis,* 1974, BKAT, 1, Genesis 1–11, 17.

herself was part and to which she gave life. It is thus a feature of both the patriarchal narratives and Ruth that they do not close around themselves but point forward to new events.

## 3.   Intertextual Reading

In recent exegetical research the concept of "intertextuality" has played a steadily increasing role. No text has come into being or is heard as an independent entity; all, it is rightly emphasized, are strands in a network of texts.[17] That a text should come into being and be understood only in the light of other texts is not a new insight. Form critics have long stressed that texts belong to definite genres, to a particular *Gattung,* which is employed in particular situations. The dirge, for example, is normally used together with texts of the same or similar kind and in situations where there are grounds for mourning. And by choosing the dirge as a genre the author can ensure that the listeners understand what is being said within the context of the dirge.

From a form criticism perspective there is therefore no doubt that a text is understood via other texts. The account of Esau and Jacob's birth belongs to the group of birth legends, and for the reader who knows the genre it will be interpreted as such. For it makes a difference whether we read Gen. 25:19–26 as a legend or regard it as a description of a difficult birth. When read as a legend the text deals with the birth of a chosen one, and all the particular features of the conception and the actual birth serve to emphasize this. In this case it is not the mother's labor pains that command attention. That might be the case, on the other hand, if the women were sitting together relating their bodily experiences of birth.

When dealing with the intertextuality of a narrative there are good reasons for starting at the same point as the form critic and finding other narratives within the same genre in order to consider similarities and differences. This is not the end of the matter, however. Above and beyond the genre we must question thematic resemblances and similar situations. We may then find that texts that the form critic judges to be largely unrelated do in fact belong to a general network. While many form critics would make a sharp distinction between a genealogy and a birth legend, from an intertextual point of view we might expect that they do in fact belong within the same network. For the point of the birth legend is precisely to give prominence to a great member of the tribe to whom the listener is probably related, or knows in some way.

The concept of intertextuality thus indicates a wider field of texts than the *Gattung,* or genre, to which a particular text belongs, and this has conse-

---

[17]Cf. Sipke Draisma, ed., *Intertextuality in Biblical Writings: Essays in honor of Bas van Iersel,* Kampen, 1989, as well as Kirsten Nielsen, "Intertextuality and Biblical Scholarship," *SJOT* 2 (1990): 89–95.

quences for the interpretation of the ending of Ruth. Here the form critic would note the difference between two such dissimilar genres as the birth legend and the genealogy and conclude that the latter is a later addition. The intertextual critic, in contrast, is interested in a possible link between the two texts and examines whether they do not in fact belong within a common network. And so where earlier research has tended to regard 4:18–22 as a later addition, more recent research is much more inclined to see a link between the narrative and final genealogy.

However, the fact that intertextuality points to a larger network of texts does create certain problems. For in theory such a network may be endless. Each and every text has come into being on the basis of a network of other texts that the author consciously draws on and wishes the reader or listener to keep in mind during the experience of the new text. But this new text is also part of other networks that the author is unaware of: for texts have a history, they are reemployed in new situations, and new listeners link them to other texts. The interpretation of texts is therefore never at an end. Yet this does not prevent us, the readers, from choosing to concentrate on finding the texts that the author has used and expects to be known to readers and listeners. In this way we can seek to understand Ruth in the context that was the author's own. That is the basic premise of this commentary.

I take as my starting point for analyzing the author's application of older traditions in Ruth the work of the American literary critic Harold Bloom. In his poetics Bloom emphasizes that what interests him are those poets who wrestle with their great forebears: "My concern is only with strong poets, major figures with the persistence to wrestle with their strong precursors even to the death."[18] Every poetic work is an erroneous reading of a previous work, says Bloom. One could also formulate this by saying that every writer wrestles like Jacob. Whom and what is fought against is up to the exegete to find out. For the biblical texts are themselves part of a long tradition and are a link in a continuous deconstruction of earlier texts. Yet the deconstruction is a reconstruction too. For from the first text the next is created, and this in turn nourishes new texts.

Bloom speaks of the poet's struggle to become himself or herself through the murder of his or her precursors. Such a parricide requires of course that both a child and a parent exist, that is, artists with a strong will and personality. And even if, in our "erroneous reading" of Bloom, we were to prefer a less violent word than "murder," such as "conversation," or "dialogue," there needs to be a writer with whom to hold that dialogue. But is it possible for exegetes today to operate with a clear line of authorial influence in the transmitted texts? Can we in other words speak without more ado of the "author" of Ruth? For our knowledge of tradition history points to a far more complex process of

---

[18]Harold Bloom, *The Anxiety of Influence: A Theory of Poetry*, Oxford, 1973, 5.

origin than that which normally lies behind a modern poem, while at the same time the trend in modern literary criticism is toward a total devaluation of the author's influence on the text.

Finally, these days even the concept of "text" is being subjected to a comprehensive[19] debate that must be taken into consideration when applying a conscious method to a text such as Ruth.

### Textual Theory in Recent
### Literary Research

Scholarship used to believe that it could discuss the meaning of a text with relative assurance. The meaning was defined as what the author wished to pass on to the listener or the reader. There has long been a consensus that this is far too narrow a definition. The matter-of-course assumption that meaning comes about when the reader meets the author's intention via the text is no longer self-evident.

The reasons for this are many, and we shall dwell only on a couple of the most important. The author is often quite inaccessible, a figure about whom we know only what can be deduced from the text. Moreover, even if we were fortunate enough to know the author's identity and had a wealth of information about his or her external circumstances and ideological attitude, it remains problematic to claim that the text contains precisely what its author has intended, let alone to assert that the text really transmits what the author believes it says, or the "intentional fallacy." In recent textual analysis, therefore, the writer plays a very limited role; in fact he or she is regarded by a number of critics as "dead" in relation to the text.

The unambiguity of the text has been submitted to scholarly debate as well. Textual analysis in recent years has not only demonstrated how language is multiple in meaning, but has also underlined the need for the reader to become involved in an ongoing interpretation of the text, as well as, it must be added, the network of contexts into which every text fits. No text can be read in isolation. Yet it was precisely this constant interplay between text and context that created the problem, for in the wake of the "death sentence" on the author came the inquisitorial question: "Is there such a thing as a text?"[20] Can we still speak of a "text" with one specific meaning, which presents itself to the reader, when all the time the text must be read in the light of other texts? Or is that which we call the "meaning" of the text simply what every reader individually brings to, and therefore takes away from, the text?

---

[19]A clear introduction to some of the theories under debate is to be found in Terry Eagleton, *Literary Theory: An Introduction,* Oxford, 1983.

[20]Cf. Stanley Fish, *Is There a Text in This Class? The Authority of Interpretive Communities,* Cambridge, 1980, 305.

### The Intertextuality
### of the Biblical Texts

This brief sketch of the postmodern situation for exegetes and literary critics can seem paralyzing. Yet it should not come as a surprise to biblical scholars that the authors of the texts we are to interpret are for the most part inaccessible; that the texts are multiple in meaning; that each one of them belongs in a network of other texts; and that reader responses are many and varied. That this is the case for exegetes is demonstrated with all possible clarity by the genesis and subsequent history of the texts themselves. The Old Testament is a work of tradition. It came into being through a lengthy process under constant reinterpretation and has given rise to a wealth of commentaries. Whoever interprets such a work must therefore have a sense of its potentiality for multiple meanings and must respect each text for such possibilities.

The conditions for interpretation outlined above have pointed to the multiplicity of language and the weaving of each individual text into a network of meaning. But the fact that a word, an expression, or a narrative contains a multimeaning potential does not mean that all of them are realized in the concrete situations where they are employed. Just as a sentence is always employed in concrete situations and contexts and gains its meaning thereby, so is a story employed in a concrete situation and is not to be read as a text subjected to every possible intertextuality. On the contrary, it is to be read precisely in the context which at the time in question, in the particular environment and in the specific situation, seems in best agreement with the text.

As readers we are not independent of our own time and surroundings. We belong a priori to one or several "interpretive communities" and therefore perceive within particular frameworks of understanding. A text is always read through other texts on the basis of particular expectations—which are either met or disappointed, but which are always present and therefore serve to limit the number of possible meanings.

The fact that the author is usually anonymous and absent (or in parts of an analytical study should be kept out of the analysis) does not mean that the author has been unable to help the reader follow the intentions he or she has had during composition. If we accept that every text is always a contribution to a dialogue with one or more earlier texts—or is an attempt to defuse a previous text—we receive through the text a steady flow of information about the intertextuality from which the author was working.

The author's help to the reader consists not only of "hints" to the previous text or texts it wrestles with. Also the "gaps" that the author has equipped the text with and which demand the reader's response can lead us in a definite direction, for example, back to the previous text.

In spite of the stress in recent years on the absence of the author and the text's lack of unambiguity we must therefore assert that communication is possible. Admittedly it is not a direct dialogue between author and reader. What we as readers relate to is "texts" in the plural, not only the concrete text before us and the texts which we have as pre-knowledge but also the texts that the author (as well as possible later redactors of the text) intends as context.

The multiple meaning of the language and the necessity of an intertextual reading are realities; but the language is, as we have seen, an applied language. And thus we are taken out of the language system and into history and society, where the dialogue takes place. As readers we enter into concrete cultural and historical contexts. But this involves us taking responsibility for our share of the dialogue.

As responsible readers we must not just be sensitive to the signals that the text conveys, but also must be open to the discussions that our own reading can raise when we pass it on to new readers. The biblical texts belong to our own culture as legitimizing texts, and function in the church institutions as the basis for true preaching. The truth, in this context, is not of a preordained kind existing independently of university research and the church's application of it.

It is thus of considerable importance which methods we exegetes employ. Some methods open us up for a dialogue about the text, while others delimit the possible meanings of a text and canonize one particular interpretation as though it were the entire truth.

The purpose in writing this commentary on Ruth is to present the interpretations that appear most likely if we attempt to read the book within a network of texts out of which it came into being. It is not my intention to offer a complete, in the sense of closed, interpretation of the work.

## 4. Literary Context

### The Author's Use of Older Traditions

A significant part of the intertextuality of Ruth consists of the traditions that the author draws on, expecting recognition among his audience. The difficulty for the modern reader, of course, is that we do not have the same background knowledge as they. There will be signals in the text that they picked up, but we no longer notice. Conversely our pre-knowledge will be marked by a whole range of later texts and experiences that were not available to them. So our interpretation of Ruth is always a reinterpretation. Nonetheless, with regard to methodology we can limit the risk of reading into a text by consciously questioning the signals that point to other Old Testament texts presumed known to the author and his audience.

In practice this means that we take explicit references such as the mention of Rachel, Leah, Tamar, and Judah as invitations to include precisely these figures from patriarchal "history" in our interpretation. In addition, we regard the thematic link between the famine and infertility in Ruth and the patriarchal narratives as a conscious signal that the book should also be read as patriarchal history.

Thus Ruth belongs within an intertextuality of women's stories that deal with infertility and the triumph over it. The most obvious examples of women who do their utmost to get a son are Sarai's use of the Egyptian Hagar as a stand-in (Genesis 16), Lot's daughters, who conceive with their father and thereby become ancestresses of Moab and Ammon (Genesis 19), and Tamar, who seduces her father-in-law, Judah (Genesis 38). The stories of Rebekah's, Rachel's, and Hannah's difficulties in having children can also be included in this context.

All these stories belong to the patriarchal narratives, but the very word "patriarchal" tempts us to overlook the crucial role that women play, and the wealth of stories testifies to their efforts. Without women there are no patriarchs.

### The Link
### between Ruth and Tamar

The clearest signal in Ruth refers to Tamar, who gave birth to Judah's twins, Perez and Zerah (cf. the blessing in 4:12 and Perez's genealogy in 4:18–22). In this context, therefore, we shall concentrate on the link between Ruth and Tamar and through this on Boaz's family background.

The main content is as follows. The patriarch Jacob's son, Judah, marries a Canaanite woman, Shua's daughter, who bears him three sons. Judah chooses Tamar as a wife for his eldest son, Er. Er however dies, leaving Tamar childless. Judah then asks his second son, Onan, to enter a brother-in-law marriage with Tamar; but he too dies, as a punishment for refusing to make his sister-in-law pregnant. There is now only one son left, the young Shelah, and Judah hesitates to give him to Tamar. She is therefore sent home to her father to wait there until Shelah comes of age. After a long wait in vain Tamar decides to gain her right by a trick. She dresses up as a prostitute, seduces her father-in-law without being recognized, and becomes pregnant by him. When her pregnancy is discovered, she presents his seal and staff as proof that it is indeed Judah who has made her pregnant. Judah admits that she has right on her side because he did not give her his youngest son; thereafter he does not touch her. At birth it transpires that she is carrying twins. After struggling in her womb for primacy both boys are born and the midwife names them: Perez, the elder, and Zerah, the younger.

The story constitutes a clearly rounded whole. It begins with Judah's family situation, including the death of his two sons and Tamar's critical situation as a childless widow (Gen. 38:1–11), and ends with the resolution of the crisis: the birth of the twins (Gen. 38:27–30). The narrative thus begins and ends with a broadly described genealogy. Claus Westermann[21] regards this as a sign that the narrative has existed in oral form as a single story.

As an independent narrative the story of Tamar deals with a resourceful woman who saves the family from demise by untraditional means. As such it reminds us of the other *stories of women,*[22] where the tragedy of childlessness is turned around and all ends happily. Our sympathy is with Tamar, without Judah therefore becoming a villain. His reluctance to hand over a third son after losing two is perfectly understandable. Nor is there any doubt that he is an honorable man, who pays his dues where possible.

The depiction of Judah's reaction when the case is solved supports the corresponding picture of the honorable man. At first, hearing that Tamar is pregnant he demands that she be punished; but when the true nature of the case is revealed, he recognizes that she is more righteous than he. Thus he is not only righteous in the sense that he demands that the law should be upheld; he is also honorable in acknowledging that necessity breaks all laws.

So the story ends happily—for both sides. Tamar becomes a mother, securing her social situation. The widower Judah unexpectedly finds his two dead sons replaced by twins full of vitality, and is thereby recompensed. Moreover, the account of the birth gives the impression that it was not just an unusual woman who became a mother, but that the younger twin, Perez, who took the place of the first-born, would also come to play a special role in the history of the family.

### The Story of Tamar as a Link
### in the Patriarchal Narratives

Read in this way the story of Tamar draws a positive picture of one of the family's famous women. But if the picture frame is changed, the picture changes character. And if a story is placed in a new context, its meaning changes. By placing the story of Tamar immediately after the selling of Joseph and before his meeting with Potiphar's wife a crucial alteration takes place.

The overall frame is the narrative of Jacob and his family. Jacob is the chosen one. Admittedly he cheats his way to the firstborn's right and blessing, but at an important point he behaves as he should. He obeys when his father Isaac orders him to marry a Canaanite woman (Gen. 28:1ff). He fathers twelve sons, but just prior to the Tamar episode he loses his favorite son, Joseph. Incon-

---

[21]Claus Westermann, *Genesis,* BKAT, 3, Genesis 37–50, 1982. Cf. also J. A. Emerton, "Some Problems in Genesis XXXVIII," *VT* 25 (1975): 338–61; J. A. Emerton, "An Examination of a Recent Structuralist Interpretation of Genesis XXXVIII," *VT* 26 (1976): 79–98; and J. A. Emerton, "Judah and Tamar," *VT* 29 (1979): 403–15 concerning Genesis 38.

[22]Cf. the feminist interpretations of stories of women in the Old Testament in Athalya Brenner, ed., *A Feminist Companion to Ruth,* Sheffield, 1993. Of particular interest here is Fokkelien van Dijk-Hemmes, "Ruth: A Product of Women's Culture?", 134–39.

solable, he sits back and thinks only of being reunited with Joseph in the kingdom of death. At the same time Joseph is sold to Potiphar.

Seen in this perspective there are features of the story of Tamar that take on a different aspect. We note that Judah mixes with Canaanites and even marries and has children with one of them. He chooses a daughter-in-law for his eldest son, and even though it is not stated directly in the text, it is likely that she too is a Canaanite.

The family is then struck down by the death of the eldest son. But surely nothing happens by chance in Jacob's family, that of God's elected? As a continuation of the account of the selling of Joseph, it is reasonable to see the son's death partly as a suitable punishment for the sorrow Judah caused his own father by making him "sonless," and partly as a consequence of Judah's having married a Canaanite woman.[23]

In similar fashion a change takes place in our understanding of the meeting with Tamar. In the original version Judah's intercourse with the disguised Tamar shows that necessity is the mother of invention. But when the story is taken together with the account of the chaste Joseph, who knew how to reject the foreign woman who would seduce him (Genesis 39), then Judah's intercourse with Tamar is seen as the opposite of chastity: quite simply, it is incest. In both cases there are persons who should not be sexually active: in the first because they are too foreign for each other, in the second because they are too closely related.

That such a reinterpretation of the story is possible and has actually taken place at a later date appears from the book of Jubilees chap. 41, which clearly reflects a negative attitude to Judah's intercourse with Tamar. Judah's deed is and remains sinful.

As demonstrated, the story of Tamar can be read very differently depending on the context. This has a bearing on the historical context of Ruth. In a situation where the link with Tamar is seen as a disqualification for the family of David, the author of Ruth returns to the positive features in the Tamar tradition, thereby creating his own picture of the ancestresses of David.

### Tamar and Ruth

The story of Tamar, as we now see, is placed in the context of the patriarchal narratives. But at the same time it must be seen as a precondition for Ruth, even though the two in the final redaction are not placed close to each other.

The woman's story that is the closest parallel to Tamar is that of Ruth. The author refers directly to Tamar when having the people of Bethlehem offer the wish that Boaz may have as many heirs as Judah with Tamar (4:12). This places the story in a context that must already be known to the listeners.

---

[23]Cf. the antipathy to foreign women in Num. 25:1–5.

Of course it is not enough just to point to a single reference from one text to the other. Intertextuality must be more comprehensive in content if it is to influence an understanding of the text. Where then is the link between such stories?

The choice of narratives in the Old Testament would suggest that stories have been retained that spoke together, that supplemented one another, that set one another in relief. Open questions in a story call for answers in the form of the next story, which again raises new questions and answers.

### *The Book of Ruth as a*
### *Response to the Story of Tamar*

The structure of Ruth is similar to that of Genesis 38. Both texts open and close with information of a family nature. In both, a critical situation arises because a young, childless woman loses her husband. But in Ruth the distress is increased by there being two childless women and a childless mother-in-law, all of whom are widows. In both texts interest is concentrated on the family of which Perez is to become the ancestor. In the story of Tamar this comes about through the birth legend, where Perez is the one who secures the birthright. In Ruth, on the other hand, we find Perez's genealogy, ending with David in the tenth generation. The texts agree that Tamar and Ruth become ancestresses; but only in Ruth are we led through Perez right up to King David.

The author of Ruth reemploys a Perez genealogy that has presumably existed in the context of the traditions of Tamar and Judah. The genealogy was the starting point, but also the problem and the occasion for creating the story (see pp. 23–28).

In both places the women are marginalized. Tamar has been sent away from her in-laws' family, home to her father, to wait for a young man whom she apparently never gets. Ruth, on the other hand, voluntarily renounces a return home to her mother and a new marriage. Instead she has linked herself to her mother-in-law, who can no longer give birth to a son to replace Ruth's dead husband. Both women elect to remain with the in-laws, but the motive of family fidelity plays a far greater role in Ruth, where her loyalty is mentioned time and again.

Ruth is also stated to have chosen Naomi's land, people, and God. The portrayal of Ruth's departure echoes that of Abram when he left his land, his family, and his father's house to go to the land that God would show him. But where Abram set off at the word of God, Ruth dares to break away with no word of any kind. The story shows, however, that this was counted to her advantage. Ruth is here depicted not just as a new and better version of Tamar, but also as a new and better version of Abram.

A corollary of being marginalized is that one can no longer use the normal channels of society to gain one's right. When women cannot acquire the necessary son by pursuing the law and demanding their right, they must resort to trickery, which is closely linked to their sexuality. Tamar is forced to take on the guise of a prostitute and seduce Judah, while Ruth must choose the plan of lying beside Boaz and asking him to lay his garment over her naked body.[24] The difference between the two is that when Ruth refers to Boaz as a redeemer, it is because she is asking for more than a single night. She wants marriage. Moreover it is probable that both are marginalized by being foreign women. In the book of Ruth, however, this motif plays a far more important role than in Genesis 38, where Tamar is never directly referred to as a Canaanite. Thus it is the foreign woman whom Yahweh chooses as ancestress for David.

Finally, it must be emphasized that in Ruth the many prayers for Yahweh's intervention make it far clearer that behind the choice of David's family stands God himself. What Genesis 38 omits to say directly receives full expression in the depiction in Ruth of how Yahweh's choice repeats itself down through this family.

The transformations between Tamar and Ruth are due not only to a need for variation. Ruth does not tell the same story as Genesis 38. It is a new and better story, which derives from the author's wrestling with a powerful precedent. Through the book the reader is convinced that it was the God of Israel who intervened when Ruth became the mother of Obed, and that Ruth was not only chosen but was worthy of the choice. Ruth thereby becomes a better background for Perez's genealogy than the story of Tamar would have been.

## The Recycling
## of the Ruth Narrative

There follows a brief demonstration of how rabbinical exegesis works in practice intertextually with Ruth by filling in many of the holes in the narrative with information from other texts.

### The Targum to Ruth

The Aramaic version of Ruth[25] is simultaneously a translation and a commentary. The Hebraic text that is its basis corresponds to the Masoretic Text. The version follows the text closely, and the few deviations from the MT reveal

---

[24]Cf. my interpretation of Ruth 3:4, 7 in Kirsten Nielsen, "Le choix contre le droit dans le livre de Ruth. De l'aire de battage au tribunal," *VT* 35 (1985): 201–12, where I show that it is Ruth and not Boaz who is naked.

[25]Cf. Étan Levine, *The Aramaic Version of Ruth*, Rome, 1973, as well as D.R.G. Beattie, *Jewish Exegesis of the Book of Ruth*, 1977, 17–18, 21.

a close connection to the Peshitta. Woven into the translation are paraphrasal sections, while for the name of God the necessary paraphrases are employed. As a textual witness the Targum is of limited value, but as a contribution to the understanding of Jewish exegesis and thinking it is indispensable.

First and foremost the Targum shows which aspects in the story have required elaboration: the narrative amplifications underline not least the legal aspects of the book. Marriage with a Moabite woman is pronounced illegal, to be punished by death (*Targum to Ruth* 1:4–5). Ruth's wish to follow Naomi is expanded with a meticulous account of the law abidance expected of a proselyte (1:16). Ruth's strength to bear the yoke of the Lord's messenger is mentioned in 3:11, Ruth is described as a proselyte in 2:6, and the concept of levirate marriage is introduced in 3:10. Boaz is presented as a righteous judge whose prayers end the famine (1:6 and 3:7). Moreover, he has prophetic gifts and can predict that Ruth will be the ancestress of kings and prophets (2:11). Boaz's self-control at the threshing floor is also underlined (3:8).

The emphasis on the role of the law in this Targum is due to its liturgical use at the Feast of Weeks, where the lawgiving at Sinai was remembered. Thus Ruth is the proselyte par excellence who subjects herself unconditionally to the law; the lesson to be learned from this is that God rewards those who are faithful to the law.

### Ruth Rabbah

Proof that detailed exegesis was not exhausted with the Aramaic versions of the biblical writings is clear from the rich literature of the Midrash.[26] The most interesting aspect of the *Midrash to Ruth*, namely, *Ruth Rabbah*, is its characterization. Elimelech is shown as a wealthy man who fled from the famine not because it was life threatening but because he was loath to help the destitute in his country. The very fact of leaving one's country without a compelling reason is regarded as a grave sin, and when this is combined with his lack of solidarity with the poor the reason for his premature death and the family's unfortunate situation is self-evident. He is guilty of his own fate.

Ruth, on the other hand, is beautifully drawn. She may not be free of unchaste thoughts, but compared to the other gleaning women she is a paragon. In this respect great emphasis is placed on her conversion, a fact which fits in well with the use of the book at the Feast of Weeks. Boaz is portrayed as a worthy representative of the righteous who resists all temptation, and as with the *Targum to Ruth* the concept of righteousness plays a major role.

Regarding interpretation there are many details of minor importance in the

---

[26]Cf. Beattie, *Jewish Exegesis*, 21–22.

elaboration of the narrative. It is worth dwelling on the origin of the Midrash, however. The basic exegetical principle is that missing information in one text can be deduced from other texts. In this way Ruth follows rabbinical thought in a constant dialogue with earlier texts, and itself provides material for later texts. *Ruth Rabbah* is therefore not a fabrication of fantasizing scribes but the result of learned rabbinical exegesis.[27]

One of the problems that rabbinical exegesis has been concerned with and that plays a decisive role in the understanding of the genesis and function of Ruth is King David's Moabite origins. *Ruth Rabbah* to 4:18 puts it thus:

> R. Abba b. Kahana commenced by citing the following verse: " 'Rage and do not sin, [commune with your own heart upon your bed and shut up!]' (Ps. 4:5).

> "Said David before the Holy One, blessed be He, 'How long will they rage against me and say, "Is this family not invalid [for marriage into Israel]? Is he not descended from Ruth the Moabitess?" '

> " ' . . . commune with your own heart upon your bed': [David continues,] 'You too, have you not descended from two sisters? You look at your own origins "and shut up."

> " 'So Tamar who married your ancestor Judah—is she not of an invalid family?

> " 'But she was only a descendant of Shem, the son of Noah. So do you come from such impressive genealogy?' "[28]

The tone is didactic. It is not denied that David is descended from a Moabite woman, Ruth. But the sting is turned on those who take offense at David's background. Are they themselves of pure descent?

### The Position of Ruth
### in the Canon

Originally the story of Ruth was an independent narrative retold on various occasions. It then acquired written form, but not until later was it placed alongside the other biblical books. In the Hebraic Bible Ruth belongs with the Scriptures. Among these the five festival rolls, the Megillahs, formed a special collection. These were used in the synagogue at the appropriate annual feast: the Song of Solomon at the Feast of Passover, Ruth at the Feast of Weeks, Lamentations at the Feast to mourn the destruction of the Temple, Ecclesiastes at the

---

[27]Tryggve Kronholm, "The Portrayal of Characters in Midrash Ruth Rabbah. Observations on the formation of the Jewish hermeneutical legend known as "biblical haggadah'," *ASTI* 12 (1983): 20.

[28]*Ruth Rabbah: An Analytical Translation*, translated by Jacob Neusner, Atlanta, 1989, 197.

Feast of Tabernacles, and Esther at the Feast of Purim.[29] Seen in this light the primary context for Ruth is the festival at which the book was used.

The use of Ruth at the Feast of Weeks was partly because the action takes place in the period between the Passover and the Weeks, during the grain harvest. But the link between the Feast of Weeks and the lawgiving at Sinai made another aspect of Ruth significant. As is apparent from the *Targum to Ruth* and *Ruth Rabbah,* Ruth was regarded by the rabbis as an exemplary proselyte. Her acceptance of Israel's God as her own and her willingness to subject herself to the yoke of the law was emphasized as worthy of imitation. Finally it must be mentioned that according to an old tradition King David was not only born during the Feast of Weeks but also died at that time of year.

Against these traditions stands another view of Ruth which finds expression in its position in the Septuagint and the other translations. Here we find Ruth placed between Judges and 1 and 2 Samuel.[30] The redactors who gathered the Old Testament texts into a continuous account of the story of God and Israel have presumably sought to place Ruth in a position where it chronologically belongs. When the author has dated the events in the book to the period of Judges it makes sense to read it as a continuation of the other accounts of the Judges' period.

When read in this context the book links up with a series of narratives dealing with women who are used and abused. In Judges 19 we read of mass rape and the abuse of a Levite wife (also from Bethlehem). Chapters 20–22 deal with the subsequent revenge against the tribe of Benjamin who were guilty of the rape and what that involves in the way of injustice—also with the women who were finally forced to marry Benjaminites. As the last verse of Judges says: "In those days Israel had no king; everyone did as he saw fit."

With this background Ruth serves as a transitional link between the period of lawlessness and the institution of the monarchy. Actually through a woman, and a foreign woman at that, the tribe which is to bear the greatest king of Israel is perpetuated. Ruth links Judges to 1 and 2 Samuel, where the introduction of the monarchy is a central theme and the rule of David a climax. But before we hear about the monarchy, Samuel's birth is related. Once again we meet the ancient theme of the woman who is infertile. Like Sarah and Rachel, Hannah has to watch her fellow wife give birth without being able to produce any children herself. She goes to the house of the Lord, laments her lot before God, and

---

[29]Originally Ruth was placed together with the other writings, in fact even first, since Samuel was thought to be its author. Then came the Psalms. When Ruth became part of the Megillahs, two differing principles were employed, partly the feast's position in the calendar, partly the chronological date. For further discussion see Edward F. Campbell, Jr., *Ruth,* 1975, 32–36, or Sasson, *Ruth,* 11–13.

[30]For further discussion as to what extent this is its original position see Robert L. Hubbard, Jr., *The Book of Ruth,* 1988, 4–7.

is rewarded with a son, Samuel, who anoints both Saul and David. Again a woman's fate plays a crucial role in the people's future. But where Ruth takes the unheard-of path of visiting Boaz at night at the threshing floor, Hannah goes to Israel's God and prays herself to a child. Common to all the stories is that a child is elected to play a special part in the history of the people.

## 5. Historical Context

### Genealogy and Narrative
### as Political Instruments

Ruth is a literary work. This fact has caused a number of scholars to refuse to admit that the book has any other function than being good literature, i.e., that it is entertaining and instructive. Thus Hermann Gunkel rejects every attempt to find a hidden agenda in Ruth. The book is apolitical, simply a beautiful story about a widow's faithfulness. Its purpose is not to legitimize the Davidic dynasty, nor is it propaganda against Ezra and Nehemiah's view of mixed marriages.[31]

To this we may respond that a text that culminates in the birth of King David must have had a political purpose when it came into being. The portrayal of Ruth's path to marriage with Boaz is formed as an election story, which like the patriarchal narratives aims to persuade the reader that behind the election of the Davidic dynasty lies God himself.

The following examination of the book's historical context will therefore take the genealogy as its starting point, as we try to establish the situation in which such a genealogy could be of benefit. We shall then look to see whether in the so called historical books of the Old Testament we can find a meaningful intertextuality for Ruth, and thereby demonstrate in what circumstances and to what purpose the book may, not necessarily must, have been constructed.

### The Origin and Function
### of the Old Testament Genealogies

Regarding historical research[32] the evaluation of the Old Testament genealogies has been marked by two different tendencies. Whereas a scholar like Heinrich Ewald regarded the genealogies as the best imaginable sources to the history of Israel, Hermann Gunkel maintained that the genealogies were literary constructions that served to create a link between persons in the individual traditions. The idea that the genealogies are reliable historical sources gave rise

---

[31]Gunkel, "Ruth," in *Reden und Aufsätze*, 88–89.

[32]See the overview of historical research in Robert R. Wilson, "The Old Testament Genealogies in Recent Research," *JBL* 94 (1975): 169–89.

to a number of critical objections. The similarity between the genealogies in Genesis and various mythological texts from the Near East therefore convinced many that the genealogies too could be used as sources for the mythological ideas of early Israel and thus cannot be employed as sources for the real history. In addition to this came the division of Genesis by literary critics into several sources, with the indication that genealogies are especially to be found in late texts such as P and 1 and 2 Chronicles and are therefore hardly reliable history.

The debate on the source value of the genealogies was kept alive by, among others, W. F. Albright and Martin Noth. Albright's stress on the importance and credibility of the oral tradition led to renewed consideration as to whether some of the genealogies might not contain historically correct information. Also of significance was Noth's distinction between those genealogies that have a purely literary purpose and have never existed independent of the narratives they are now linked to, and those which have had a previous independent existence and can therefore be accounted of value as source material.

These nuances also characterize recent contributions to the debate. In pursuing Gunkel's line Marshall D. Johnson[33] points out that many of the genealogies have been employed to show Israel's link to its neighbors (e.g., Gen. 19:36–38; 25:12–16; 36; see also Genesis 10), or were created to link originally independent traditions regarding Israel's origins. He adds that the purpose of Genesis 10; 11:10–26, and Ruth 4:18–22 has been to cover periods in Israel's history where no accounts were available, while the genealogies in Genesis 5 and Genesis 11:10ff. have formed the basis of chronological speculations. The genealogies in 1 Chronicles 2–8, on the other hand, are based on military lists and have had a political function, just as some genealogies (partly in 1 Chronicles, partly in Ezra-Nehemiah) have been used to legitimize the right to certain public offices. In addition to this the genealogies have been employed to some extent as a demonstration of the purity of the postexilic community. Johnson thus made it clear that genealogies can have different functions.

The political purpose of the genealogies has been powerfully supported in anthropological quarters. Robert R. Wilson[34] distinguishes between three spheres where genealogies are used. The first is the family, considered through biological ties. The second is the politico-religious sphere, where, for example, the segmented genealogies (genealogies that carry on several lines) can be used to express the political power relationship at the time in question. In a so-

---

[33]Marshall D. Johnson, *The Purpose of the Biblical Genealogies, with Special Reference to the Setting of the Genealogies of Jesus,* 1969, 77–82.

[34]Robert R. Wilson's brief presentation in his article from 1975, "Old Testament Genealogies," *JBL* 94 (1975): 169–89, is developed in detail in his book from 1977 (Robert R. Wilson, *Genealogy and History in the Biblical World,* 1977).

ciety with a monarchy, however, there is a tendency to use linear genealogies as legitimation for the occupation of office. As a third factor Wilson specifies the religious sphere.[35]

Since genealogies function in different areas and can undergo changes so as to agree with the actual power structure, a society can operate with internally differing genealogies, each of which serves a purpose. The realization that genealogies are not passed down in order to preserve historical facts but to reflect a contemporary power structure means that they must be regarded as valuable sources for these power struggles, but do not necessarily transmit correct facts about the tribal and family relationships.[36]

### The Genealogy in Ruth

Surprisingly, Wilson has not analyzed the genealogy in Ruth, merely mentioning it as an example of a linear genealogy of the type that is often used to legitimize a king's claim to the throne.[37] In our context, however, this remark is interesting, for how can the story of a marriage between the Moabite Ruth and the Israelite Boaz have served as a legitimation of David's right to the throne?

As has been demonstrated, genealogies have their function in a concrete society. As relationships change, they can undergo major or minor revisions to ensure their continued relevance. They thus reflect tensions in existing societies at various times, and in their creation and presentation show how the attempt has been made to give status to various persons or groups. We might well imagine that rival genealogies existed for so prestigious a figure as King David, some of them emphasizing his descent from the wealthy Boaz of Bethlehem and others pointing to the black spots in his career: the descent through both Ruth and Perez, i.e., a foreign woman whose ancestress seduced her own father and a man conceived through incest. And if we then ask who might want to promulgate such a tainted genealogy, the answer is: opponents of the Davidic dynasty.

According to the Old Testament, which is our only source of information for possible royal succession disputes in the early monarchy, relations between Saul and the ambitious David were stretched to the limit. Members of Saul's family had an immediate interest in making David's path to the throne as difficult as possible, just as they could see an advantage in defaming David and his family after his succession in order to promote their own family again.

---

[35]Cf. Wilson, "Old Testament Genealogies," 180–82.

[36]Cf. an example of a recent, very positive evaluation of the source value of genealogies in Gary A. Rendsburg, "The internal consistency and historical reliability of the biblical genealogies," *VT* 40 (1990): 185–206.

[37]Wilson, *Genealogy and History*, 195.

If Saul's family were to compete over genealogies, they would probably have pointed to David's doubtful line of descent. In contrast they would maintain Saul's pure line through wealthy people in the tribe of Benjamin and a name that suggested he had been born as the answer to many a prayer, just like Samuel.[38]

Similarly the circles supporting the traditions of Samuel, the charismatic judge and prophet, would have wanted to promote their own interests by stressing the particular events surrounding Samuel's conception and birth (1 Sam. 1), thereby legitimizing Samuel's family as the elect of Yahweh of the tribe of Ephraim, and counting Joseph among their ancestors. If this is the case, the author of Ruth has also been competing with the story of Samuel's birth and has therefore had to create an equally powerful birth legend.

The Deuteronomists not only reject Saul's family, but in practice Samuel's too, as the final version of 1 and 2 Samuel proves, with David emerging as the victor. But individual accounts in the books may well have had an independent function before they became part of the historical work. They may have been part of a local power struggle in which various opponents of David's family had done their best to promote their own virtues in contrast to David's vices.

The author of Ruth is clearly not an opponent of David. On the contrary, the book can be interpreted as a conscious reaction to the smear campaign against him, the point being that everything the rivals regard as suspicious about the history of David's family points in fact to its special election by Yahweh.

The inclusion of Ruth's Moabite origins and Boaz's descent through Tamar via Perez as a significant ingredient in the Ruth narrative suggests that knowledge of David's family relationships was so widespread that the facts could not be denied. The strength of the opponents' argument was that contemporary opinion not only knew their claims to be true but also regarded them as damaging.

So the attacks on David's family had to be taken seriously. What his supporters could do was to supplement his genealogy with a story that could present a completely different twist to the unusual origins; instead of denying them they simply reinterpreted them. Thus the author of Ruth had to take up a stance both on David's link to Judah and Tamar through Boaz and to the Moabites through Ruth. It is not just his Moabite background that is the problem, as previous scholars would have us believe.[39] The link to Judah and Tamar is equally compromising.

The Moabite origins of David's family are regarded by a number of scholars

---

[38]The name Saul better suits the etymology in 1 Sam. 1:20 than the name Samuel.

[39]Cf. the following quotation in which it is clear that Jacob Licht regards the Moabite Ruth as the problem. "It [the book of Ruth] endeavors to show how the apparently reprehensible female ancestor has been absorbed into the thoroughly respectable family of Boaz in a perfectly proper way, and for irreproachable reasons." Jacob Licht, *Storytelling in the Bible*, Jerusalem, 1978, 125.

as historical fact. As evidence of this David's flight to Moab after the break with Saul is often cited. In Mispe he is granted asylum for his parents by the Moabite king (cf. 1 Sam. 22:3–4). A. A. Anderson[40] believes that in the time before David became king, it was part of the family's tradition that it had foreign origins. Anderson defends the historical correctness of this with the argument that no one later would have thought of giving David a foreign ancestry. Thus, once he had gained power, the royal house had to form the family tradition into a suitable story to show its foreign origins in a more favorable light. This took place under David or Solomon, perhaps shortly after the division of the kingdom. Anderson further assumes some reworking of the material in the period of Ezra and Nehemiah, when the problem with mixed marriages becomes acute, and so the redactor has sought to turn Ruth's marriage into a levirate marriage.

Anderson's division of the book's origins into such phases, where external circumstances have required certain revisions in principle, harmonizes with recent anthropological research. At first it is the family alone that is interested in David's origins. But when he is chosen as king, his genealogy suddenly takes on political significance. Now his family relationships can be used by his opponents in the struggle for power, and so the beautiful story of Ruth and Boaz is created to show off David in a more flattering light.

Anderson's demonstration of the need to elaborate the traditions surrounding David's origins seems convincing. What is harder to determine is at what point the political situation gave rise to such a book as Ruth.

If we are to outline a possible context on the basis of Old Testament accounts, then the last years of David's reign spring to mind, when succession disputes and revolts could be fertile ground for such literary activity.

Another possibility is the power struggle between Rehoboam and Jeroboam which led to the so-called division of the kingdom. According to 1 Kings 12 the whole nation gathered after Solomon's death to make Rehoboam king. But the rebel Jeroboam, who clearly acts as a rival to the Davidic dynasty (cf. the account in 1 Kings 11:26ff.), then returns home to participate in the negotiations with Rehoboam on a more moderate policy. The talks break down, and the Israelites reject Rehoboam with the words:

> What share do we have in David,
>   what part in Jesse's son?
> To your tents, O Israel!
> Look after your own house, O David!
>   (1 Kings 12:16)

From this we can see that it is David, Jesse's son, whom the people will have nothing to do with and not just the person Rehoboam. The derisive sentence

---

[40]A. A. Anderson, "The Marriage of Ruth," *JSS* 23 (1978): 172–73.

about looking after his own house fits in well as part of a campaign against Rehoboam. His house, the family of David, is not worth having a share in. If the tribe of Judah stands by him, then that is its problem.

In Ruth there is no attempt to hide David's membership in the tribe of Judah through Boaz. But it is characteristic that the book skirts round the division into tribes and appeals to the patriarchal traditions in its argument. It is the same God who chose the patriarchs, who now stands behind David and his house. This can be seen as an attempt to oppose the split that Jeroboam's policy had created in favor of a common Israelite people under the leadership of David's family. That the book seeks to appeal to all tribes is perhaps best seen in its final scene where the women speak of Obed as being renowned not just in Bethlehem.

Moreover in 1 Kings 11:26ff. we see how the prophet Ahijah of Shiloh announces to Jeroboam that Yahweh has chosen him to be leader of the ten tribes after Solomon's death. Even though the Deuteronomists in the main condemn Jeroboam, they nevertheless pass on some of the traditions that must have belonged in the circle around him and his court. Thus the traditions concerning "the division of the kingdom" show that there were powerful figures speaking up for Jeroboam and not for the Davidic dynasty.[41] Yahweh's choice of Jeroboam meant at the same time a promotion of Joseph. Like the prophet Samuel Jeroboam was an Ephraimite and thus belonged to the tribe of Joseph (1 Kings 11:26). A similar raising of Joseph's status in relation to Judah is known from the Genesis traditions, where he is depicted as a chaste man, in contrast to Judah, who committed incest with his own daughter-in-law (Genesis 38–39).

Finally, the portrayal of Rehoboam's journey to the ancient shrine at Shechem, where he apparently had to agree to negotiate in relation to the northern tribes, proves that the position of David's family was not a matter of course.

A comparison of the versions of the Deuteronomists and the chroniclers shows the degree to which the chroniclers allow themselves a theological arrangement of the material. Almost everything that can belittle the hero David is omitted, though not Judah and Perez's genealogy (1 Chron. 2:3ff). This points either to certain realities being incontrovertible, or to David's family relations being no longer seen as damaging but — on the contrary — a sign of election, just as Ruth maintains. This would fit in well with the glorification of David that the chroniclers presented.[42]

---

[41]Robert L. Hubbard believes that Ruth cannot be dated to the period of Jeroboam's seizure of power precisely because no writer would dare to write directly against the Yahweh oracle. See Hubbard, *Book of Ruth,* 42–43. This view is not tenable, however; the Deuteronomists clearly maintain both traditions.

[42]In his analysis of the genealogies in 1 Chron. 1–9 Manfred Oeming has shown how that of Judah is structured around that of David. See Manfred Oeming, *Das Wahre Israel: Die "genealogische Vorhalle" 1 Chr. 1–9,* Stuttgart, 1990, 100–130.

We must dwell briefly on the fact that the story of Ruth does not have the David ideology as its basic premise. On the contrary, the account of Ruth and Boaz is created at a point when the ambitions of David's family are exposed to vehement criticism, and his supporters therefore need to turn the most vulnerable points in his family history into something positive. Thus it is not the family link to David that legitimizes Ruth, but rather Yahweh's blessing of Ruth's struggle to survive that gives the fragile dynasty the legitimation it so desperately needs.

It must further be emphasized that the story of Ruth has not been supplemented with a genealogy, as many scholars believe. The genealogy is in fact its basic premise and starting point. Admittedly the genealogy is a problem, but within the very problem lies the solution. It simply requires that Ruth be read intertextually, i.e. in the light of—among others—the Tamar narrative. Through his story of the Moabite Ruth the author creates a new story about how God has chosen David's ancestresses—not just Ruth, but before her Tamar, Rachel, and Leah. By depicting the choice of Ruth as a variation on the election of Tamar and her son Perez, and by adapting Perez's genealogy so that David becomes the tenth branch on the trunk, the author creates a new patriarchal story. Just as God chose Tamar to be the ancestress of both Boaz and David, so it is God himself who has chosen David's Moabite ancestress, Ruth, and therefore David himself is chosen![43] This is where the story of Ruth must convince its contemporary audience. And a possible time for such a presentation is the period around the division of the kingdom.

The crucial point, however, is not whether the arguments for this dating are stronger than those for another situation where the dynasty needed a defense. As we know, the only written source for the early monarchy is the biblical texts, so we must be very reticent in concluding actual history from biblical narrative. But we can use the accounts in 1 and 2 Samuel and 1 and 2 Kings to sketch out typical political situations when it would be meaningful to form the history of David's family, as is the case with the story of Ruth and Boaz. Put another way, we can point to a possible intertextuality which may be a productive background for the creation of the text that we know today as the book of Ruth.

It follows that by including a further group of Old Testament texts in the framework for understanding Ruth we are able to specify the author's purpose with the book, which we can summarize as follows:

To tell of the election of Ruth and thus of the family of David in such a way

---

[43]It would be amusing to know more about the stories that women have told through the ages to glorify their ancestresses. How would Bathsheba have told the story of David's family as she sat in the women's house—she who herself was regarded as a foreign woman, the wife of Uriah the Hittite?

as to make Ruth's story a reinterpretation of how God in his time elected the patriarchs.

The book then becomes a defense of this family's claim to the royal throne.

### *Dating*

There used to be a widespread understanding that Ruth was written in the postexilic period as a contribution to the disputes about mixed marriages. The story of an Israelite's marriage to a Moabite would recommend a milder practice than that which comes to light in the books of Ezra and Nehemiah.[44]

More recent scholarship rejects this view, one of the main reasons being that David plays a far greater role than such a dating permits. Most recent interpretations therefore agree that the book in some way has David and his family as its purpose and must therefore be dated to the preexilic period. Murray D. Gow[45] believes that Ruth was written actually during David's reign, where it served to defend his Moabite origins. Against this it can be argued that a defense of his right to the throne does not necessarily have to be written during his reign. Also during the reign of his successor, Solomon, Ruth would be an influential book in support of the Davidic dynasty.[46]

Arguments for dating Ruth must rest partly on an evaluation of the book itself, partly on the Old Testament depiction of the monarchy and the struggle for the throne. Consequently the disputes that led to the dissolution of the community between the tribes in the north and south must also be taken into consideration as a possible intertextuality for the book. Its legitimizing of David's right to the throne shares the same traditions found in 1 Samuel 15–2 Samuel 5.[47] Both accounts purport to defend David's right above all tribes, and it is therefore also probable that they too have come into being around the same time, shortly after Solomon's death and the break between the northern and southern tribes.

Also the reigns of Hezekiah and Josiah[48] have been suggested, since both kings showed an interest in incorporating the northern tribes into their king-

---

[44]Cf. the survey in Jean-Luc Vesco, "La Date du Livre de Ruth," *RB* 74 (1967): 235–47, and Gow, *Book of Ruth*, 183.

[45]In his epilogue, 207–10, Murray D. Gow (*Book of Ruth*) even ventures the thought experiment that the author is David's prophet, Nathan!

[46]Thus Campbell, *Ruth*, 28, suggests that the book was orally produced under Solomon and written down in the 9th century B.C. See also Hubbard, *Book of Ruth*, 46, who points to the reign of Solomon as after all the most likely date of composition.

[47]Jakob Grønbaek dates the story of David's path to the throne to the time of Rehoboam, in other words shortly after the division of the kingdom. Jakob Grønbaek, *Die Geschichte vom Aufstieg Davids (I Sam. 15–II Sam. 5) Tradition und Komposition*, Copenhagen, 1971, 277.

[48]Both possibilities are seriously considered by Gow, *Book of Ruth*, 201–2, but finally rejected. However, Sasson, *Ruth*, 250–52, supports the reign of Josiah with its glorification of David, a period when he believes 1 and 2 Samuel were also written.

doms and therefore may very well have needed the story of Ruth to consolidate the Davidic dynasty.

Among those scholars who still support a postexilic date is Christian Frevel, whose motive is the outward/homeward journey that fits in well with the exile experience.[49] An even later date is given by Erich Zenger,[50] who thinks that the final version of the book belongs in the second century B.C.E. Zenger underlines its messianic aspect and sees it as promoting the Hasmoneans' political and religious ambitions.

It would therefore seem that much current scholarship regards the defense of the Davidic dynasty as the key to understanding the book's purpose, and thus as a means to dating it. The majority prefer a preexilic date, but agreement ends there.[51]

The difficulty of dating Ruth is due not only to the large number of political situations that could give rise to a defense of the Davidic claim but also to the book's very form and content. Several scholars have tried to date it on the basis of language, style, environment, theology, and legal usage. But the arguments have proved to be untenable.[52] Attempts to prove a later date, based on certain Aramaisms or an archaic style or current legal usage, have slowly crumbled, and recent research generally agrees on a preexilic date.

Finally, it needs to be emphasized that even though all scholars do not agree on a date, there is a widespread understanding that the author is to be found within the royal court. The court provided not only the essential financial resources but also the environment that could produce an artist of the caliber of Ruth's author.

## 6. Theological Themes

The discovery that Ruth was originally written to champion the right of David's family to the throne does not of course exhaust the significance of the book. The effect that it had testifies to its having been read in many other situations than political power struggles. Like all works of art it is not a book with a single message for a limited time and circumstance but belongs in a network of texts that each underline particular themes in the narrative.

The book contains very few statements that could be construed as theological. Only twice does it mention God as intervening. In 1:6 Naomi has heard

---

[49]Christian Frevel, *Das Buch Ruth*, 1992, 34.

[50]Zenger, *Das Buch Ruth*, 28.

[51]Cf. Susan Niditch, "Legends of Wise Heroes and Heroines. II. Ruth" in *The Hebrew Bible and its Modern Interpreters*, ed. Douglas A. Knight, Gene M. Tucker, Philadelphia, 1985, 451.

[52]For a thorough treatment of the arguments for and against both a pre-exilic and a post-exilic dating see Sasson, *Ruth*, 240–52; Gow, *Book of Ruth*, 183–206, and Hubbard, *Book of Ruth*, 23–35.

that God looks after his people and feeds them. And in connection with Ruth's marriage we hear that Yahweh "enabled her to conceive" (4:13). But with these two verses the author also characterizes the chief feature in the book's image of God: Yahweh provides bread and babies. In this way the theology corresponds precisely to the plot, where famine and childlessness are overcome through Ruth's marriage to Boaz and the birth of the desired son.

In one other place the author makes it clear that God is behind events, when of all the fields available for gleaning Ruth "found herself working" in Boaz's field. Just as Naomi has only heard—but not yet experienced—that God has looked after his people, so it is with the meeting in the field: one senses but does not see a divine hand. If we compare Ruth with the patriarchal narratives, it is also noteworthy that God is silent. Nowhere in the book does God speak to man or woman. Nor is there a direct meeting with God—no dreams, no angels.

The fact that we can still speak of Yahweh playing a central role in the book[53] is due to the position he assumes in the dialogues. The sheer number of times he is mentioned (1:8–9, 13, 17, 20–21; 2:12, 19–20; 3:13; 4:11–12, 14) creates an awareness of his never-failing presence, whether it be disaster striking, or dearth turning to wealth. The book can thus be read as homage to the God who performs his will despite all obstacles.

However, it is not only the use of the name of Yahweh that witnesses to his presence. One of the fundamental motifs is Yahweh's care for people in need. Even though Elimelech's family was dying out at one point, it was this very family that was chosen to become the family of David. God's election and guidance of the patriarchs is repeated. And it is also this care that Naomi and Boaz appeal to when they ask for God's blessing.

Characteristic of both Naomi and Boaz's prayers is that they regard the blessing as God's natural response to human faithfulness and goodness. Naomi prays that Yahweh will give her daughters-in-law security in a marriage (1:8–9) and that Yahweh will bless Boaz (2:19–20). In both cases the goodness and faithfulness of the recipients are referred to. Boaz too prays that Yahweh will reward Ruth for her faithfulness to his people and will bless her (2:12; 3:10).

The theology of the book of Ruth finds expression not only in the prayers but also in their fulfillment. Chapter 4 can thus be read as a fulfillment of Naomi and Boaz's prayers as well as the witnesses' prayers for fertility and procreation for both Ruth and Boaz. All three parties are rewarded with what they have prayed for when Boaz marries Ruth and Yahweh enables her to conceive and bear a son. Precisely the mention of Yahweh's name in connection with the prayers serves to create tension in the book. For sooner or later Yahweh will without doubt fulfill these prayers; yet how will this come about?

---

[53]See Hubbard, *Book of Ruth*, 67.

God guides and controls events, but from beneath the surface. For on the surface itself the main characters live and move and try to form their existence as best they can. However, it is worth noticing that their plans are never fully coordinated. Ruth's wish to follow Naomi is in direct contradiction of Naomi's advice. And Naomi's passivity on her return to Bethlehem is countered by Ruth's initiative in providing food. When Naomi plans the meeting at the threshing floor, Ruth agrees to obey her, yet still she does what she sees fit. Boaz also accepts when Ruth asks for marriage; but he must take a detour before Ruth's plan can become Boaz's plan and in the end come to fruition.

Perhaps the most important point in this context is that Boaz and Naomi never meet and make plans together. According to the norms of the time it would otherwise have been natural for the two older family members to get together and plan the future of their families. But that does not happen. Each of them thinks their own thoughts, and out of all these individual plans grows a unity that leads the reader to sense that in this way God's plan is being carried out. With a fine irony, however, the author shows that the main characters do not themselves know about this interaction between divine guidance and human action.

The most refined example of this hidden interplay between human action and God's control is in chapters 2–3, where Boaz prays that Ruth may receive her full reward from the God of Israel under whose wings she has sought shelter. Little does he know that Ruth will shortly ask *him* for shelter under his own "wings" (cf. the wordplay on wings and the corner of Boaz's garment in 2:12 and 3:9). It soon turns out that it is Boaz himself who is to fulfill his own prayer for Ruth, for thus will the God of Israel show his faithfulness toward the family of Elimelech.

Through prayer the belief is expressed that Yahweh will reward human faithfulness and goodness, *ḥesed,* by showing his own *ḥesed.* The portrayal of God is marked by a clear expectation that Yahweh, who has made a pact with the patriarchs to lead and protect them, will continue to live up to his commitment as the God of the covenant. That is precisely why Naomi formulates her complaint as an accusation against the Almighty who has struck her down with such unreasonable force (1:20–21).

The concept of *ḥesed* constitutes a significant theme. In Ruth it does not denote the expectation of measure for measure to be found in the wisdom literature, but the extraordinary kindness that Ruth and Boaz offer to a family member in need. It requires courage to exceed expectations and break norms, but both are rewarded in the end. The demonstration that *ḥesed* can require a person to choose the unexpected and not just be satisfied with what the law declares also means that the women in the narrative occupy a special place.

Naomi's plan for a meeting at the threshing floor and Ruth's execution of the plan are the book's central initiative. The women break contemporary

norms and are rewarded for doing just that. Thus God is presented as being on
the side of the marginalized, conducting their case even where the law is inad-
equate and they must resort to trickery to gain justice.

Read as continuation of the final chapters of Deuteronomy, Ruth is clearly
a contrasting text. Whereas the women in Judges 19–21 are exposed to vio-
lence and attack, and no God intervenes to help them, Ruth presents two
women who despite loss and hardship are part of Yahweh's redemptive plan —
as more than passive victims. Naomi does not accept in silence what the
Almighty has done to her, but gives voice to her anguish and forms it as a
charge. She makes plans for the future and puts them into practice. Nor does
Ruth succumb to a hopeless future, but dares with all her might to carry on the
family which she had bound herself to through marriage to Mahlon.

This contrast between Judges 19–21 and the book of Ruth also underlines
how the latter makes its contribution to the stories of women in the Old Testament. Ruth is in dialogue with other women's destinies, most notably those of
Lot's daughters, Tamar, Rachel, and Leah. But the stories of Sarai and Hagar,
Rebekah and Hannah are also part of this network. Ruth thus lends her name
to a story that offers a future to the marginalized, for she is elected to be the
ancestress of one of Israel's leaders.

Ruth dates the events to the period of the Judges and the transition from a
form of government that can be characterized as lawless because it was king-
less (Judg. 21:25) to a government that through most of the Old Testament is
regarded as the ideal, namely monarchy. We can see how the author establishes
this transition in the form of a repetition of the patriarchal years, when the people lived under Yahweh's guidance and promise that they would become a
great nation and own much land. Such a theme must have found a sympathetic
response in situations where fellowship between the tribes was at a crisis, as
well as during the exile when hopes of returning home and starting a new life
were intense. During the exile it would have been a great comfort to hear how
despite great loss and hardship Elimelech's family left their "exile" in Moab
and returned home to Judah. Ruth would have given the exiles the confidence
that Yahweh was still fulfilling the prayers that people prayed and was still in
control of events.

As a liturgical text at the Festival of Weeks there is another theme in Ruth
that comes to the fore: her conversion. Just as Naomi decides to return to Bethlehem, so Ruth also returns home when she chooses Naomi's land, people, and
God. Her true home is the Israelite-Jewish community, for whom she becomes
a shining example of the foreigner who as a proselyte undertakes to live as the
God of Israel requires.

Many scholars have rightly emphasized this decision of a foreigner to join
the Israelite-Jewish community, seeing in it a link between Ruth and other Old
Testament texts that present God as God of the whole world, such as the book

of Jonah.[54] Seen from this intertextual angle the conversion motif and God's goodness to foreign peoples are clearly present. That this perspective is also part of the image of God found in the patriarchal narratives is clear from the words to Abram in Gen. 12:1–3, where Abram is not only himself blessed, but where the culmination is reached in the promise: " . . . all peoples on earth will be blessed through you." From a messianic point of view these words could just as well apply to David's ancestress, Ruth.

## 7. The Text

In language and style Ruth reminds us of the patriarchal narratives in Genesis. Only in a few places does the language diverge from classical Hebrew. In 3:3 an old feminine form is used in the 2d pers. sing., and there are a number of examples of the use of an old feminine dual suffix.[55] The use of the so-called "paragogic *nun*" is likewise often regarded as expressing an old, possibly archaic style.[56] Conversely, some scholars have alleged a number of Aramaisms that would point to a later date for composition.[57] (For a discussion of the date of the book see p. 29.)

Ruth is both well-written and well-preserved. The only textual emendments required are in 4:4, 5, 21. In a few places a decision must be made whether to read the consonant text (ketib) or the vowel text (qere), namely 2:1, 3:9, 12, 14; 4:5. A particular problem is raised by 4:4–5, where the choice of the textual basis is of crucial importance for a unified interpretation.

With the discovery of the Qumran texts it became possible to follow textual developments in the book several centuries back in time.[58] The variations in the Qumran version are extremely limited, however, and have no bearing on the interpretation of Ruth.

### The Septuagint

Most important among the old translations of Ruth is the LXX.[59] This is a very literal translation, which shows that the translator has a good knowledge

---

[54]Cf. Sasson, *Ruth*, 246–47.

[55]A few scholars believe that this is a masculine plural suffix being used of women. In favor of the feminine dual suffix, however, is that in all seven places the form is used in connection with two women: 1:8 (twice), 9, 11, 13, 19; 4:11 For a discussion see Campbell, *Ruth*, 65.

[56]Found in 2:8, 21, and 3:4, 18. Cf. ibid., 97.

[57]Cf. the rejection of this argument in Campbell, *Ruth*, 24–26 and Sasson, *Ruth*, 244–46.

[58]See Campbell, *Ruth*, 40–41, who discusses the most important variants. See also Hubbard, *Book of Ruth*, 2–3.

[59]For further discussion of the origin of the LXX see Campbell, *Ruth*, 36–40; Sasson, *Ruth*, 9–10; and Beattie, *Jewish Exegesis*, 9–10.

of Hebrew and Greek. An important detail in the LXX is its version of the name Elimelech as Abimelech. A further, minor point is that in some places the LXX adds the name of the person in question rather than the relevant pronoun. The importance of the LXX is first and foremost in connection with 4:5.

### The Peshitta

The Syrian translation of Ruth is far freer than the Greek, and it is unlikely that it draws directly on the LXX. On the other hand, it is worth considering whether this translation has not been partly revised at some point on the basis of the LXX. The translator's knowledge of Hebrew fails here and there, and at times he tries to improve the text in a homiletic style. Thus it is Ruth who is sensitive about her reputation in 3:14, not Boaz; and the reason for the redeemer refusing to marry Ruth is given as lack of faith (4:5).[60] In 1:12, presumably out of delicacy, the Peshitta omits to mention that Naomi is considering the possibility of getting a man "this night." Here the Peshitta matches the LXX. Similar mention should be made of 3:4, 7, where the Peshitta quite simply omits the words "uncovers herself."

For an interpretation of Ruth the Peshitta is helpful in a few places. Its rendering of 2:7 as "she has been gleaning since early morning even unto the rest period"[61] differs so much from the LXX's "she has not rested in the field a little" that the translator cannot possibly have used the LXX but must have translated directly from the Hebrew. The Peshitta must also be included in the interpretation of 4:5, where the translation, just like the LXX, reads *qere*.

### Vetus Latina

This Latin translation is known from a relatively late manuscript (9th century C.E.)[62] and from liturgical books and quotations by the church fathers. As regards Ruth there are few places of interest in the interpretation, primarily the threshing floor scene (3:4, 7), where according to Vetus Latina, Ruth does not uncover Boaz but covers herself.

### The Vulgate

Jerome's translation of the Old Testament is often given prominence because of the translator's knowledge of Hebrew. But even though the Vulgate

---

[60]See also Gerleman, *Rut—Das Hohelied,* 1965, 3–4, and Beattie, *Jewish Exegesis,* 10–17.

[61]Cf. Beattie, *Jewish Exegesis,* 12.

[62]See Jesus Cantera Ortiz de Urbina, *Vetus Latina—Rut: Estudio critico de la version latina prejeronimiana del libro Rut, segun el manuscrito 31 de la Universidad de Madrid,* Madrid/Barcelona, 1965, 46–47.

in principle is translated from the original language, we must not overlook the fact that Jerome to a great degree drew on the LXX. The Vulgate can therefore only be used as an independent witness of a Hebrew text form when it differs from the LXX, as is the case in 4:5.

# RUTH

# I. THE HUSBANDS DIE IN MOAB, AND RUTH AND NAOMI RETURN HOME TO JUDAH

## Ruth 1:1–5

### After living in Moab ten years, Elimelech and his sons die

1:1 Once during the time of the Judges there was famine in the land, and a man traveled from Bethlehem in Judah to the land of Moab in order to live there as a foreigner with his wife and his two sons. 2 The man was called Elimelech, his wife was called Naomi, and his two sons were called Mahlon and Chilion. They were Ephrathites from Bethlehem in Judah, and they came to the land of Moab and stayed there. 3 Then Elimelech, Naomi's husband, died, and she was left alone with her two sons. 4 They married Moabite women; one was called Orpah, the other was called Ruth. They lived there for about ten years; 5 but then both Mahlon and Chilion died, and the woman was left alone without her two boys and without her husband.

[1:1] Chapter 1 consists of three parts: vv. 1–5, vv. 6–18, vv. 19–22. The first part introduces the misfortune: famine and death, and forms a contrast with the happy ending in chapter 4, where Ruth marries Boaz and through her son becomes the ancestress of the family of David. The second part describes the journey from Moab to Bethlehem with Ruth's confession to Naomi's God as its climax. The third part deals with the homecoming to Bethlehem and Naomi's lament. Through this the misfortune motif is maintained, and vv. 19–22 therefore form a contrast to the women's joy in 4:14–17.[63]

The book of Ruth begins by placing the story at a specific period in time (for a detailed discussion of the importance of time indications for the book's structure and tempo see the Introduction, pp. 2–5). From the start the reader is given to understand that the following story deals with events from the past, events that took place "once during the time of the Judges." The author makes no men-

---

[63] A closer analysis of the structure of chap. 1 is to be found in Gow, *Book of Ruth*, 27–40.

tion of any particular judge, so the purpose of the time indication can hardly be
to identify a precise point in a chronological span, but is rather to place Ruth
within a certain group of texts. Through the immediate placing of the story in
time the reader is led into a network of stories to which Ruth also belongs,
namely the narratives found in Judges.

The tale of Ruth and Naomi must be read in the light of the traditions from
the time when the God of Israel called heroes forth to deeds of war and helped
the tribes to conquer and retain the land. We are dealing with the tremendous
events that led to the creation of the people of Israel, as well as to the rape and
abuse of innocent people, to the abduction of women and to general lawlessness (Judges 19–21). For at that time there was no king in Israel, and every man
did as he pleased (Judges 21:25). The reader's curiosity is stimulated. Are we
about to hear a tale of injustice and lawlessness or about God's intervention on
behalf of his people through the creation of something new?

It is not only the introductory dating of the book that signifies the context into
which it is to be read. Also the LXX's placing of Ruth immediately after Judges
underlines this. In this canonical context the story of Naomi and Ruth comes to
form a dialogue with the last chapters of Judges. Chapters 19–21 depict the im-
potence of women, whereas Ruth tells of how even a foreign woman such as
the Moabitess Ruth can be chosen by Yahweh to save the family of David.
Through this foreigner the new institution of monarchy is created in Israel.

On the other hand the reference to a famine that forces the main characters
out of Judah does not point to traditions from the period of Judges, and Judges
itself offers no example whatsoever of famine. However, the traditions of the
patriarchs and their wanderings do (Gen. 12:10; 26:1; 41:54). Of particular interest are the Abram traditions, which speak not only of famine but also of
childlessness, two themes that are inextricably linked in Ruth. But where the
problem in Ruth is that the husbands are dead, it is formulated differently in
the Abram traditions.

In Genesis 12 Sarai is assimilated into the Egyptian Pharaoh's harem and can
very easily become pregnant with the wrong man, with the result that it is not to
the continuation of Abram's family that she contributes. And in a later story
Abram, on Sarai's advice, becomes the father of Ishmael, but with the wrong
woman, the Egyptian Hagar (Gen. 16:21). In the Abram traditions it is neither
the foreign man nor the foreign woman who is to carry on the family; in Ruth by
contrast it is precisely the *foreign* woman who is to be the ancestress of David.

According to Gillis Gerleman the famine is a literary motif that has nothing
to do with reality. The climate was so similar in Moab and the Bethlehem area
that there would hardly have been a serious crop failure in the one without it
affecting the other. Christian Frevel by comparison[64] believes that there can be

---

[64]Cf. Gerleman, *Rut*, 14, and Frevel, *Das Buch Ruth*, 46.

considerable differences in the amount of rainfall in Judah and Moab, making the description in 1:1 completely plausible for the reader.

Gerleman is right in thinking that famine is a literary motif in the Old Testament; but it is important that the mention of Moab as the place to which the family can flee to survive has seemed plausible when based on the experiences of the times. If the reader wonders why Elimelech chose Moab, the reason is not that the climate was similar. Rather, what the reader was being asked to consider was whether it was wise to mix with the Moabites at all (cf. Genesis 19; Numbers 25).

The reference to a famine serves to remind the reader of similar accounts elsewhere. Just as Abraham, Isaac, and the sons of Jacob had to go abroad to find the necessary food, so Elimelech and his family are forced away from their own country. Now they have to live as refugees in Moab and experience insecurity in foreign parts. The similarity between Elimelech's fate and that of the patriarchs nonetheless gives the reader the hope that there are not only parallels in the misfortunes but also in the subsequent joys. Just as the patriarchs' lives continued after the famine and left deep furrows in the history of the people, so will the destiny of Elimelech's family form itself. What the reader still does not know is how this will come about.

The starting point is the town of Bethlehem in Judah. As the name the "House of Bread" suggests, it is well-known as a fertile area; but this selfsame place is struck by its opposite, a famine. Moreover, Bethlehem is a place to which a number of positive traditions are linked, including the stories of David, whose father was from Bethlehem (1 Sam. 16:1). And in Micah the messianic expectations are linked to precisely this town.

Whereas Judah and Bethlehem signify that Ruth belongs in a network of texts about the good king, the land of Moab in Israelite consciousness has a negative ring. According to Gen. 19:37 the Moabites were descended from Lot and his eldest daughter and are thus the result of an incestuous relationship. That anything good could come out of Moab therefore requires further explanation. From a literary perspective it is very much one of the purposes of the book to explain this more closely. The reference to Moab functions as a marker in the text, raising a question that requires an answer. But the marker contains its own answer, provided we include the intertextuality toward which it points.[65] Through the reference to Moab and thus indirectly to the tradition of Lot's daughter, the reader is given the opportunity to consider the story of Ruth

[65]Cf. Tryggve N. D. Mettinger, "Intertextuality: Allusion and Vertical Context Systems in Some Job Passages," in *Of Prophets' Visions and the Wisdom of Sages: Essays in Honor of R. Norman Whybray on his Seventieth Birthday,* ed. Heather McKay, 1993, 264, who speaks of the markers in a text having a double character. With a quotation from Riffaterre the function of the markers is further explained: "They are both the problem, when seen from the text, and the solution to that problem when their other, intertextual side is revealed."

and Naomi as an ancestress story, which deals with two women's surprising recourse to self-help in order to save the family from extinction.

Scholars who regard the mention of Moab as purely geographical information will see it as an expression of historical knowledge about actual circumstances. They will therefore refer to the tradition that at one point David brought his parents to safety with the king of Moab, which should testify to the fact that David's family actually came from that area (1 Sam. 22:3–4).[66]

In the course of the first few verses both time and space are created for the story. The travel motif is introduced and the reader now has two well-known places to relate to: Bethlehem in Judah and Moab abroad. But the prevalent view of the two places is no longer valid. The fertile "House of Bread" is struck by famine, while the foreign Moab has became a place of asylum. This inversion of the normal situation not only sets the action going but creates a tension in the text that makes us wonder whether Moab really is better than Bethlehem. Will Elimelech in fact settle there or is the outward journey merely a precondition for the real purpose: the homeward journey? (See Abram's outward and homeward journeys in Gen. 12:10–20.)

[2] Just as geographical information can point to the network of texts through which a story is to be understood, so personal names can also give information that helps to a better understanding of the narrative. Thus they can anticipate the course of events: *Nomen est omen.* The name Elimelech means "God is king" or "My God is king."[67] The name thus sets out the king theme, which is the end point of the book: David. Elimelech's wife is called Naomi, i.e. "my joy" or just "sweetness," but she refers to herself later as Mara, i.e. "bitterness" (1:20). This double naming reflects the development through which the action moves, from Naomi lamenting her suffering before the women in Bethlehem to the point where she again stands among them with the newborn child in her arms.

Elimelech and Naomi have two sons. Stories about two sons are widespread and often have as their point the success of the one and failure of the other, and thus a rivalry in their relationship. (See Cain and Abel, Ishmael and Isaac, Esau and Jacob.) In this case, however, the reader's expectation of a drama between brothers is swiftly disappointed. Both sons die without heirs, and thus they must both be assumed to be out of the story (see 4:10, however).

Their names immediately create the same impression. Mahlon can be translated as "sickness" or "infertility," while Chilion means "consumptive."[68] It is

---

[66]Thus, for example, Gerleman, *Rut,* 8, who thinks that the link between David and Moab is very much the historical nucleus of the story, in fact the reason that Ruth came to be written.

[67]For a closer discussion of the meaning of the names in Ruth see Sasson, *Ruth,* 17–19, and Martin Noth, *Die israelitischen Personnamen im Rahmen der gemeinsemitischen Namengebung,* 1928.

[68]Cf. Sasson, *Ruth,* 18–19. See also Campbell, *Ruth,* 53–54, who deems it impossible to decide what the two names mean.

striking that neither of these names is found elsewhere in the Old Testament,[69] which could suggest that the author has specifically named Elimelech and his family with a view to the story about to be told. The LXX renders Elimelech's name as Abimelech, possibly because this name is better known. Whatever the reason, this version takes the reader of the LXX back to the patriarchal narratives. Here we are told how both Abraham and Isaac come into contact with the Philistine king, Abimelech (Genesis 20–21; 26). The Elimelech family belong to the Ephrathah family in Bethlehem (cf. Micah 5:2, "But you, Bethlehem Ephrathah, . . . you are small among the clans of Judah"; 1 Sam. 17:12 and Ps. 132:6).

Thus Ruth begins with the essential information about the family that the reader is soon to meet, just as it closes with a series of family particulars in the form of a genealogy. Such a circular composition creates a roundedness and a continuity that is also familiar from the patriarchal narratives. The Abraham story begins in similar fashion, with Abram's departure from his homeland and the sparse information about his closest family. Then comes an account of a number of events, and regularly throughout Genesis details are given in the form of genealogies as to how the family is progressing.

[3–5] Like many other stories Ruth takes as its starting point a situation of want, in this case the famine that forces the family into exile. The want increases when the head of the family, Elimelech, dies—leaving his wife and sons to fend for themselves. Hunger and death thus become the negative conditions for a significant leitmotif in Ruth: *bread and life*. No mention is made of the cause of Elimelech's death. Later traditions could not allow such an event to remain unexplained, however, and have interpreted his death as a just punishment for leaving his homeland and failing to show solidarity during the famine (see Introduction, p. 18).

Life for widows, orphans, and foreigners was regarded in the Old Testament as extremely insecure; this is mirrored among other things in the repeated requests to look after these groups. In Ex. 22:20ff, for example, there is a prohibition against the exploitation of foreigners, and the threat of divine punishment is made if the widow and the fatherless are abused. The same thing happens in prophetic exhortations, as in Isa. 1:17, 23, where the prophet prescribes that his contemporaries look after the cause of the widow and the orphan. Unable to imagine better conditions in Moab than in Israel the reader will therefore draw the conclusion that the situation for Naomi and her two sons is now the worst possible: living alone in a foreign country.

---

[69]The name Elimelech, however, is known from other West Semitic languages; for example, it is found in an Amarna letter from Jerusalem as well as in texts from Ugarit. Cf. Campbell, *Ruth,* 52.

Whereas Elimelech in vv. 1–2 is the central figure (a man traveled . . . with *his* wife and *his* sons), now it is Naomi who assumes the main role (Elimelech is described as *Naomi's* husband and the two sons as *her* sons), hinting at the importance of women in the following events. Not until chapter 4 does the focus move back to a man, Boaz.

The sons' marriage to Moabite women involves both a stabilizing of the situation in Moab but also the risk of a crisis. On the one hand the family now has a chance of surviving; on the other hand it may be lost to Israel forever (cf. the story of Abram and Sarai at the court of the Egyptian king (Gen. 12:10ff) or the parallel stories in Genesis 20; 26).[70]

The text itself contains no evaluation of the sons' marriage; it simply states it as a fact, leaving the reader to consider whether the following events are a consequence of their marrying foreigners. The names of the two Moabite women are difficult to interpret. According to rabbinic tradition Orpah gets her name from turning her back on her mother-in-law (from *'rep,* neck). D.R.G. Beattie interprets Ruth as "the one who satiated (root *rwh*) Naomi with her kindness."[71]

The information about the names of the two sons and their wives forms a chiasm: Mahlon, who is mentioned first, is married to the last-mentioned of the women, Ruth, as can be seen from 4:10, where she is described as Mahlon's widow.

With the mention of the marriages comes the expectation of the continuation of the family and assimilation into the Moabite community. But ten years of infertility pass,[72] after which the two sons die. The sons are mentioned here as boys, despite the fact that they are adult men. The reason is hardly a wish to increase sympathy for the poor widow, who has lost her young sons. The author is extremely reticent with this kind of thing. But with the unusual usage of the word *yeled,* the narrator can create a connection between the situation here which deals with death and 4:18, where the word is repeated when Naomi takes a new boy, *yeled,* in her embrace and experiences the truth that life continues.

In 1:5 life is still threatened, however, for all that remain on the stage are three widows. The original lack of daily bread is replaced by an equally crucial lack of successors. Naomi is now not only a foreigner who has fled from famine, she is also a childless widow. The crisis appears all-encompassing.[73]

---

[70]Cf. also the fact that cohabitation with Moabite women could have serious consequences (cf. Num. 25:1–5). Ruth's Moabite origins have created problems for the rabbinic scholars, since the law in Deut. 23:4–7 forbids fellowship with both Moabites and Ammonites. But since the law spoke of these foreigners only in the masculine gender, it was interpreted as a sign that the prohibition did not include Moabite women.

[71]Cf. D.R.G. Beattie, "Ruth III", *JSOT* 5 (1978): 46. Gerleman, *Rut,* 14f thinks that neither Orpah nor Ruth are symbolic names, but genuine Moabite female names.

[72]The ten years of infertility are not finally counterbalanced until ten generations are born into the world, according to 4:18–22.

[73]On the basis of the action the section ends here. For further discussion of Murray D. Gow's demarcation of the chiastic structure ending in 1:7b, see the Introduction, p. 3.

# Ruth 1:6–18

### When Naomi wishes to return home,
### Ruth clings to her, but Orpah leaves

1:6 Then she broke up with her daughters-in-law to return home from
the land of Moab, for in the land of Moab she had heard that Yahweh
had looked after his people and given them bread. 7 She left the place
where she had lived, and her two daughters-in-law accompanied her,
and they set off to return home to the land of Judah. 8 But Naomi said
to her daughters-in-law: "Return home now, each to your mother's
house! May Yahweh show you[a] goodness, just as you[a] have done to the
dead and to me. 9 May Yahweh grant that you find comfort, each in
your husband's house!" Then she kissed them; but they broke into
tears. 10 And they said to her, "We want to return home with you to your
people." 11 Naomi answered, "Return home now, my daughters! Why
do you want to go with me? Are there still sons in my womb that you
can marry? 12 Return home, my daughters, go now; I am too old for a
man. And even if I thought there was hope for me, and even if I belonged to a man tonight and actually had sons, 13 should you wait until they become adults, should you refrain from finding a husband? No,
my daughters! It is more bitter for me than for you, for Yahweh's hand
has struck me down." 14 Then they broke into tears again, and Orpah
kissed her mother-in-law; but Ruth clung to her. 15 Then she said,
"Your sister-in-law is returning home to her people and her God. Follow your sister-in-law!" 16 But Ruth answered, "Do not make me leave
you and return home without you. No, where you go, I will go, and
where you live, I will live; your people are my people, and your god is
my god. 17 Where you die, I will die, and there I will be buried. Yahweh strike me down again and again, but only death will separate us!"
18 When she saw that she had made up her mind, she gave up trying to
persuade her.

a. These suffixes in the 2d person plur. are probably old dual forms in the feminine
and not masculine plur. See also 1:9, 11, 13, 19, and 4:11.

[1:6–7] From the infertility of Moab the scene switches to the fertility of
Judah, where Yahweh again has provided the essential conditions for life. The
outward cause is not man-made but controlled by the God of Israel. The text
does not explain the sudden cessation of famine. The Targum to Ruth 1:6 and
3:7 does, however, giving the reason as Boaz's intercessory prayers for his

people. Together with her daughters-in-law Naomi now leaves the land that
has provided her with daily bread over the years but has also claimed the lives
of her husband and sons. She wishes to return home to Judah (note that the
key concept *šûb,* return home, is used no less than twelve times in this chapter).[74] The obvious question at this point is: What role are the Moabite daughters-in-law to fulfill in Judah? Will they be a help or a hindrance for Naomi's
future?

The fact that help is on the way is clear from the statement that the God of
Israel looks after his people. The verb "to look after" is employed in similar
fashion for the sending of rain to the land in Ps. 65:10, but it is also used in
Gen. 21:1 and 1 Sam. 2:21, where God helps infertile women to conceive
(Sarah and Hannah). Could this also be part of Yahweh's purpose for the
Moabite women? Bethlehem has again become the "House of Bread," to which
Naomi therefore wishes to return, but will God also look after her daughters-
in-law, who are not of his people?

[8–10] The answer seems to have been found when Naomi urges the two
women to return to Moab; the future in Judah is for Naomi alone, not for the
Moabite women. Most scholars are surprised by the phrase "mother's house"
rather than the traditional "father's house" (cf. Gen. 38:11, where the childless
widow, Tamar, is sent back to her father's house). However, the expression
"mother's house" is found in Gen. 24:28, where, just as in Cant. 3:4; 8:2, it reflects the central role of the mother in everyday life.[75] And after all it is not so
surprising in the circumstances that the natural alternative to a life abroad with
their mother-in-law is a life at home with their own mother. As the story moves
on, we also begin to realize that the most important areas of the action are
linked to women and their world. For instance, Naomi does not turn to a male
relative to ask him to find a new husband for Ruth, but she takes matters into
her own hands.

It is clear that she believes she is doing the best for them. Her blessing centers on the word *ḥesed,* which denotes partly God's goodness to the daughters-
in-law, and partly their goodness to their late husbands and Naomi. *ḥesed* signifies faithful goodness, i.e., constant care. The word is repeated in crucial
situations (2:20 and 3:10) and constitutes an important theme in the book (see
further discussion in the commentary on 3:10). Naomi wants the God of Israel
to take care of the two women, but immediately the care is defined as married
security. The word security, *měnûḥāh,* alludes to a home where one can live in
peace with the day-to-day essentials taken care of. It is no longer a question of

---

[74]Ruth 1:6, 7, 8, 10, 11, 12, 15 (twice), 16, 21, 22 (twice).

[75]See Carol Meyers, "Returning Home: Ruth 1.8 and the Gendering of the Book of Ruth," in
*A Feminist Companion to Ruth,* ed. Athalya Brenner, Sheffield, 1993, 85–114.

their mother's house but of "each husband's house"; that is, where the adult woman is blessed, according to the text. But Ruth and Orpah refuse; they would rather follow Naomi back to her own people.

No mention of their motives for doing so is adduced, but this is characteristic of the narrative form. By giving such priority to dialogue in the story, the author allows readers to form their own image and opinion of the protagonists, withdrawing and allowing the characters to act and their readers to form their own conclusions.

There are other literary forms the author draws on to keep readers attentive. When Naomi's good wishes for her daughters-in-law take the form of a prayer that the God of Israel will show goodness to them, the reader's expectation is that Naomi will be heard. In this way the author moves the story on by creating tension as to the outcome. When, and not least how, will Yahweh fulfill her prayer?

**[11–13]** Naomi elaborates her reason for sending Ruth and Orpah home. Even if she herself could find a husband and bear sons for them to marry, it would be unreasonable for the daughters-in-law to have to wait until they were grown men. The conclusion must therefore still be that there is no future for them together with her.

Naomi's concern about their waiting so long for husbands is thematically linked to one of the motifs in the Tamar story and must be read in this intertextuality (for a discussion of the close link between Ruth and the Tamar story, see the Introduction, pp. 13–17). In Genesis 38 we are told that having lost two husbands Tamar is waiting in vain for the youngest brother-in-law to come of age and marry her. This, we are led to believe, must not be the fate of Ruth and Orpah.

Whether Judah's fear of giving his son Shelah to Tamar is also to be read intertextually with Naomi's reaction is difficult to decide. But Naomi's anxiety to say goodbye to Ruth and Orpah may well be due to the experiences she has had with them. Neither of them can have children, it would seem, and both have lost their husbands. Perhaps Moabite women are dangerous for Israelites?[76] If so, there is good reason to insist that they return home.

The marriage of a childless widow to a brother-in-law to allow her to remain within her late husband's family is a well-known phenomenon in the Near East. In the Old Testament such a marriage is called a levirate marriage, and detailed rules for it are to be found in Deut. 25:5–10 (see also the section on levirate marriage on pp. 84–85).

For an understanding of the action so far it is important to underline that at this juncture Naomi rejects the possibility of a levirate marriage for Ruth

---

[76]Regarding this motive see Danna Nolan Fewell and David Miller Gunn, *Compromising Redemption: Relating Characters in the Book of Ruth,* Literary Currents in Biblical Interpretation, 1990, 72–74, Cf. also Gen. 19:30–38 and Num. 25:1–5.

*brother of deceased man is obliged to marry the widow.*

and Orpah. Every reasonable consideration points to their future being back home in Moab. That Naomi has a corresponding future in Judah is not mentioned. On the contrary, Naomi herself points out that it is her whom Yahweh's hand has struck (a similar notion that misfortune comes from the hand of God is to be found in Job 19:21 and 23:2). Her life has been destroyed, and there is nothing to suggest that things will be different even if she leaves Moab.

[14–15] As we noted in the previous section, "There was once a man who had two sons" is a familiar start to a story illustrating how different sons can be. "There was once a woman who had two daughters-in-law." It now turns out that the two who have hitherto worked as a unit are also different. The author briefly dismisses Orpah, whose name is not even mentioned; suddenly she is as anonymous as the unnamed redeemer in 4:1. And, just as the redeemer serves as background to Boaz's declaration that he will marry Ruth and produce an heir for Mahlon, so does Orpah function as a contrast to Ruth's declaration that she will stay beside Naomi. Neither Orpah nor the redeemer acts wrongly; but their refusal makes Ruth and Boaz's actions all the more meritorious.

It is characteristic that the author passes no judgment on Orpah, leaving this to the reader. Sooner or later a reader is bound to react negatively. Thus in the Midrash *Ruth Rabbah*[77] we find the brutal account of Orpah on her return journey being raped by a hundred men and a dog.[78] Here we are left in no doubt as to what to think of Orpah, though according to the narrator of Ruth she does only what her mother-in-law insists on.

So whereas Orpah takes the consequences of Naomi's words and kisses her goodbye, Ruth does the opposite. She clings to Naomi and refuses to leave her. In Hebrew the root *dbq* is used, which is known from Gen. 2:24, where, however, it is used about the man who is to leave[79] his father and mother and cling (*dbq*) to his wife. Seen in this light Ruth's gesture is just as crucial for the future as a man who marries.

For the third time Naomi speaks, urging Ruth to follow her sister-in-law and return to her people and her god. The word for god is the same as that used for the God of Israel, and is a plural form. It can therefore also be rendered as "her gods."[80] Naomi has so far argued on the basis of their marriage chances in Moab, but talk of a new husband only makes Ruth cling to Naomi as if the two

---

[77]For further discussion of *Ruth Rabbah* see the Introduction, pp. 18–19.

[78]Cf. Kronholm, "Portrayal," *ASTI* 12 (1983): 33–34.

[79]The word for "leave" in Gen. 2:24 is found again in Ruth 1:16.

[80]The Moabite god Kemosh appears to have the same position in Moab as Yahweh in Israel, so also in his case the plural form should be translated by the singular. Cf. Sasson, *Ruth,* 29–30.

of them belonged together. Further reasons for returning are required and
Naomi now stresses Ruth's ties to her people and her religion.

**[16–18]** Instead of allowing herself to be persuaded Ruth now takes Naomi's
arguments and responds to them. It is Naomi she wishes to be together with and
not a new husband. Therefore Naomi's people and God shall be her people and
God. They shall live together and be buried together, for only death can part
them. In content this has the same effect as a declaration of love in which a young
man or woman declares their love and plights their troth (cf. Cant. 8:6–7).

Ruth's answer falls naturally into rhythmic sentences with recurrent
forms—poetry that has appealed to generation after generation. In Jewish tradition these are the very words that are used as an example for the proselyte to
follow. That Ruth is seen as the prototype of a proselyte is already clear from
the *Targum to Ruth* 1:16, where Naomi explains to Ruth the demands of the
law on the convert. In the *Targum to Ruth* 2:6 Ruth is described as a proselyte,
while in connection with Ruth 3:11 she is said to be strong enough to bear the
yoke of the Lord's law.

In the context of the story Ruth's declaration of love is a definitive break with
the past in Moab and a transition to an unsure future. But where Naomi's attitude in 1:13 is an expression of hopelessness, Ruth's is more difficult to sense.
Is this the defiance of desperation? She who has been married to an Israelite
man, a foreigner, has she really nothing to return to in Moab? Will she be an un-
welcome burden in her mother's house? Or should we rather take the repetitive
use of "you," "your people," and "your God" as signs that it is precisely Naomi,
her people, and her God who will be able to create a future for Ruth?

The description of Ruth's abandonment of Moab also places the story in the
genre of patriarchal narratives. Behind this account lies the story of how
Abram left his native land, family, and father's house (Gen. 12:1). But where
Abram leaves with a trust in God's promise that he will acquire a land and become a great people, Ruth leaves her land without a promise from any God regarding her future.[81] All she has to hold on to is Naomi, who is trying to push
her away. And God is silent.

Is Ruth's faith not greater than Abram's? In Gen. 15:6 we read that Abram
believed the Lord, and the Lord credited it to him as righteousness. Nothing
similar is said of Ruth. The author does not formulate God's attitude with an
editorial gloss but allows the sequence of events to show that it was credited
to Ruth's righteousness, for from her King David himself was descended.

Is Ruth's faith greater than Sarah's? one might also ask. For even though
Sarah in Gen. 17:15–16 is given that very name as a sign that she will be "the
mother of nations," and even though she listens to the prediction that she will

---

[81]Cf. Phyllis Trible, *God and the Rhetoric of Sexuality,* 1978, 173.

bear a son within a year (Gen. 18:10), she does not believe it but laughs at the very thought.

Ruth's decision to follow Naomi is strengthened finally by an oath in which she swears by the God of Israel and uses his name, Yahweh. At the start of the dialogue between Naomi and her daughters-in-law Naomi expressed the wish that Yahweh would show them *ḥesed*. At the close of the dialogue it is Ruth who takes the name of Yahweh onto her lips. In this way the conversation is rounded off; but where Yahweh at the start is linked to a continued existence in Moab, by the end it is the new life in Judah that he is to bless.

Ruth has bound herself by oath and the final word has been spoken. The purpose of the whole declaration, according to Gillis Gerleman, is to present the judaization of the foreign woman as convincingly as possible. Now she is to leave her people and join the Israelite people juridically and religiously in a new context that comprises the most important elements in life: land, grave, people, and faith.[82]

Naomi's reaction to Ruth's declaration is ambiguous. On the one hand she abandons her attempt to dissuade Ruth and bows to her wishes, on the other hand there is not a single word in the chapter to show that Ruth's love is returned, or even that Naomi just accepts her company. Her silence creates a tension in the story that leads the reader to ask how this unusual relationship can possibly develop.

# Ruth 1:19–22

### On arrival in Bethlehem Naomi laments her loss
### to the townswomen

1:19 Then the two of them proceeded to Bethlehem. But when they came into Bethlehem, the whole town was in turmoil because of them, and the women said, "It is Naomi!" 20 But she said to them, "Do not call me Naomi, call me Mara, for the Almighty has made life very bitter for me. 21 With full hands I left here, but Yahweh has caused me to return home empty-handed. Why do you call me Naomi, when Yahweh has witnessed against me, and the Almighty has brought misfortune over me?" 22 This is how Naomi returned home together with Ruth, her Moabite daughter-in-law, when she came home from the land of Moab. They came to Bethlehem at the start of the barley harvest.

[1:19–21] So the two arrive in Bethlehem.[83] The narrative style here is even more terse than in the renowned travels of Abraham and Isaac in Gene-

[82]Gerleman, *Rut*, 20.
[83]Verse 19a is often placed in the previous section, cf. Gow, *Book of Ruth*, 30–38.

sis 22, where they at least go together and talk together on the way to the place of sacrifice. While silence seems to characterize Ruth and Naomi, the sight of them sets tongues wagging among the women of Bethlehem, who to their joyful surprise recognize Naomi.[84] In contrast, not a word is said of Ruth, either by the women or by Naomi, who speaks only of her own unhappy fate. The cue word is her name. She no longer wishes to be called Naomi, i.e., "my joy" or "sweetness," now that her fate is better covered by the name Mara, i.e., "bitterness."

Naomi comes straight out with the complaint that her hardship is not a mere caprice of fortune. It is God the Almighty who has embittered her life (cf. Job 27:2). She left Bethlehem with full hands but returns with them empty. It may seem surprising that Naomi left "with full hands" considering that the reason for her departure was a famine. Such a concern doubtless lies behind the statement in *Ruth Rabbah* that Elimelech did not leave his land because of want but because he was a wealthy man and did not wish to share his wealth with others. He and his family were subsequently punished for this.

On the other hand Naomi may also be referring to the fact that she departed as a married woman with two sons. Now she is a childless widow. That she has a daughter-in-law with her apparently makes no difference. Not until the end of the story do we discover that the same Ruth who is included by Naomi under the complaint of empty-handedness proves to be worth more than seven sons (4:15). "Mara" is therefore no lasting substitute for "Naomi."

By twice calling her God "the Almighty" Naomi underlines that in her opinion her misfortune has been sent by God. In the context of the patriarchal narratives, where the name of God "the Almighty" is found a number of times in the Priestly traditions,[85] Naomi's words can be seen as a signal to the reader that whatever has happened or will happen, it is God himself who is behind it. The book of Ruth is also *Führungsgeschichte*. But the fact that this does not rule out death and misfortune is clear from both the patriarchal narratives and from the other biblical work where God is regularly referred to as "the Almighty," namely the book of Job. This too treats the question of how the Almighty deprives a man of his property and children only to restore everything for the best in the end.

Using the legal term "witness against," Naomi turns herself into the accused, in no less a case than one where the Almighty is the accuser. What Naomi does not know, and never finds out, is what God has accused her of. On this point she really does resemble Job, who likewise does not know why one

---

[84]Cf. B. Jongeling, "HZ'T N'MY (RUTH 1, 19)," *VT* 28 (1978): 474–77, who argues that the reaction is formed not as a question but as an expression of positive surprise.

[85]Cf. Gen. 17:1; 28:3; 35:11; 43:14; 48:3; 49:25; see also Ex. 6:3.

misfortune after another suddenly rains down upon him. We are tempted to ask whether in fact Naomi is yet another example of the innocent sufferer.

[22] The chapter ends with a stage direction aimed at both Naomi and Ruth. It is spelled out yet again that Ruth is a Moabite and that they have come from Moab. This too indicates the direction of coming events as the Moabite Ruth meets the Israelite community. No one must expect that her decision to share country, people, and God with Naomi has changed her status. She remains a Moabite. What has changed, on the other hand, is the external situation. When Naomi and her family left Bethlehem, there was famine in the land. When they return, the barley harvest is about to begin. The literary and narrative beauty of this balance forms a brilliant climax to the background for what is to follow, allowing the reader to take pause before plunging into the events of the next chapter.

# II. RUTH GLEANS
# IN BOAZ'S FIELD

# Ruth 2:1–3

### Naomi consents to Ruth's plan to glean

2:1 Naomi had a relative[a] on her husband's side, a wealthy man of Elim-elech's family; he was called Boaz. 2 The Moabite woman Ruth now said to Naomi, "I will go out into the field and glean behind the one[b] I win the favor of." And she replied, "Go then, my daughter!" 3 So she left, and she came out and gleaned in a field behind the harvesters. And it so happened that the field belonged to Boaz, who was of Elimelech's family.

a. Qere reads: a relative. Ketib denotes an acquaintance. Since it is clear from the context that Boaz belongs to Elimelech's family, qere must be the most likely reading.

b. Jack M. Sasson reads the text differently, linking the masculine suffix to Boaz and taking Ruth's proposal as a question: "Should I go to the fields and glean among the ears of grain, in the hope of pleasing him [Boaz]?"[86]

[2:1] Chapter 2 falls into three parts: vv. 1–3 take place in the morning in Bethlehem; the events of vv. 4–17 occur during the day out in Boaz's field; while vv. 18–23 describe Ruth's return home in the evening in Bethlehem. The chapter is structured through a series of dialogues and has as a significant motif the food (bread and grain) that Ruth needs for Naomi and herself, which Boaz gives her.

Like chapter 1 this chapter begins with information of a family nature. Elim-elech has a relative who is a rich landowner. The contrast between the family's wealth and the empty-handed Naomi's situation is underlined, but the mention of a wealthy relative creates the expectation that perhaps help is at hand.

In a community based on joint solidarity it is the family that is the safety net to which the weak can turn. Whether the concept *mišpāḥāh* here refers to what we would today call a clan or a family is impossible to decide.[87] The im-

[86]Sasson, *Ruth*, 38, 42–43.

portant thing is the solidarity that the concept denotes for the reader. While Naomi was among foreigners in Moab with neither husband nor sons, here in Bethlehem there is a point of contact through her deceased husband. The question now is whether this relative will live up to the hopes that the mention of his name encourages.

The final piece of information about him is his name, Boaz. D.R.G. Beattie interprets it through the Arabic verb meaning "to be shrewd";[88] but even if this meaning should be known to the reader, the signal is not unambiguous. For if Boaz is a shrewd man, will he use his shrewdness to Naomi's advantage, or is he rather the sort of man who will exploit his intellectual strength to his own advantage?

Another possible interpretation is that "Boaz" means "in him is strength." Such a popular etymology possibly lies behind the LXX's rendering of the name as Booz, which can mean exactly that.

[2–3] The next item in the chain of information concerns Ruth. She reacts to the fluent situation with a concrete proposal to secure the daily bread—at least for a time. Ruth will glean (a key concept in this chapter) in the harvested fields, if she can find a place where the owner will show her favor. Jack M. Sasson links the 3d pers. masc. suffix to Boaz and interprets the situation to mean that Ruth asks Naomi whether she should try to please Boaz by gleaning in *his* fields. Against this it must be pointed out that the narrator still holds open the question of where Ruth is going to glean, and deliberately formulates it imprecisely as "the one I win the favor of." This is clear from the emphasis in v. 3 on coincidence: "it so happened" that it was Boaz's field. There is no question of a deliberate plan—from Ruth's side, that is.

Ruth is spoken of here as the Moabite woman, drawing attention to her weak status. The practice of gleaning behind the harvesters is mentioned in Old Testament legislation (Deut. 24:19), where the foreigner, the fatherless, and the widow are allowed such a right (see also Lev. 19:9; 23:22). Care for the weaker members of the community is a general feature of legislation in the Near East. In the Ugarit texts it is part of the king's office to secure the rights of the widow and the orphan: "Daniel . . . Is upright, sitting before the gate, Beneath *a mighty tree* on the threshing floor, Judging the cause of the widow, Adjudicating the case of the fatherless" (*ANET,* 151). The introduction to the law of Hammurabi similarly emphasizes that Hammurabi's task is "to cause justice to prevail in the land, to destroy the wicked and the evil, that the strong might not oppress the weak" (*ANET,* 164).

The formulation in Ruth, however, shows that she must first win the owner's favor, which is not just a matter of course. This can also be seen from

[87]See Sasson, *Ruth,* 40.
[88]Beattie, "Ruth III," 46.

the prophets' repeated criticism of social conditions (Amos 5:10–15; 8:4–6; Micah 3:1–3; Isa. 1:21–24; 5:8–13; see also the entreaty to look after orphans and widows in Isa. 1:17). In this context favor must mean permission to glean.

The initiative is Ruth's, and Naomi approves the plan without more ado. By now she is calling Ruth "my daughter," which shows her acknowledgment that she and Ruth belong together. What happens in the future will be of importance to both of them.

In v. 3 we are told briefly and to the point that Ruth does precisely what she planned. There is a difficulty, however, in the text apparently stating that she goes straight to work, for this would presuppose that she has every right to go out to a field and glean irrespective of the owner's goodwill. The reader is unsure and therefore waits to see how the owner will react.

Jack M. Sasson discusses the problem and interprets the text to mean that Ruth only prepares to glean. But the natural understanding of the three parallel verbs must be that, having talked to Naomi, Ruth leaves, goes out to the field, and gleans.

It now transpires that it is Boaz's field that Ruth has come to. The expression "it so happened," *wayyiqer miqrehā*, is only known from one other place — Eccl. 2:14f., where it denotes the fate that humankind does not control. It strikes the wise and the foolish alike. Similarly in Ruth 4 the author wishes to underline the fact that what happens now is not the result of human planning. Ruth does not inquire of Boaz directly, just as Boaz has not approached Naomi since her return, even though she is the widow of his relative.

All in all it is remarkable that Boaz and Naomi never meet in the book. Each plays a crucial role in the action; but even though the narrative is built up through a series of dialogues, the two never speak together. The author indirectly shows that although Ruth and Boaz overcome many obstacles on their way to becoming the ancestors of David, the result is not the work of Naomi and Boaz; it is because Yahweh has willed it so (see also Introduction, p. 31).

"It so happened" does not therefore mean that there is no plan behind the meeting. On the contrary, many a scholar has pointed out that the phrase must be taken as an indirect reference to God himself standing behind the apparently chance encounter. A possible parallel is the description in Gen. 24:12, where Abraham's servant is to find a wife for Isaac. At the well, before he meets Rebekah, he prays to Yahweh that today his task will "happen" (the root *qrh*), i.e., succeed. The prayer shows clearly who is expected to be behind the happy outcome of events.

This brief section begins and ends with a chiastic construction stressing the family tie between Elimelech and Boaz: "a wealthy man of Elimelech's family; he was called Boaz . . . Boaz, who was of Elimelech's family." The events that follow are to be understood within this framework.

# Ruth 2:4–17

## Boaz shows favor to Ruth

2:4 Boaz was just coming from Bethlehem, and he said to the harvesters, "Yahweh be with you!" and they answered, "Yahweh bless you!" 5 Then Boaz asked the farm hand who was supervising the harvesters, "That girl there, who is she?" 6 The farm hand who was supervising the harvesters replied, "She is a Moabite woman, the one who came home together with Naomi from Moab. 7 She asked, 'May I gather and glean among the sheaves after the harvesters?' And she started and has been going since this morning right up till now—she has only sat down for a moment in there."ᵃ 8 Then Boaz said to Ruth, "Listen here, my girl, you are not to go and glean in any other field; do not leave here, but stay with my girls. 9 Keep an eye on whereabouts in the field they are harvesting, so you can follow along after them. I will tell the farm hands that they are to leave you in peace. And when you get thirsty, you can just go over to the jars and drink from what the men have poured out." 10 Then she threw herself on the ground and said to him, "How is it that I have won your favor, that you acknowledge me, even though I am foreign?" 11 Boaz answered her, "I have been told about all that you have done for your mother-in-law after your husband's death, how you left your father and mother and your native land and traveled to a people whom you did not know beforehand. 12 May Yahweh repay you for what you have done, may you have the full reward of Yahweh, the God of Israel, under whose wings you have sought shelter!" 13 Then she said, "May I win your favor, Lord! You have comforted me and spoken to your maidservant's heart, though I am not even like one of your maidservants." 14 At mealtime Boaz said to her, "Come over here and eat some bread; you can dip your piece in the wine vinegar." So she sat with the harvesters, and he passed her some roast grain. And she ate and was satisfied and even had to leave some. 15 When she got up to go and glean, Boaz gave his farm hands these instructions: "She may also glean among the sheaves, and do not harass her! 16 You can also pull stalks out of the bundles for her and let them lie so that she can gather them; and do not threaten her!" 17 So she gleaned in the field until evening. And when she had threshed what she had gathered, there was about an ephah of barley.

---

a. The last four words of the verse present difficulties. A literal version would be, "this is her sitting the house a little." The LXX freely renders in the context, "she has not rested a little in the field." This however introduces a negative that does not exist in the Masoretic Text, and the vocalization of *šibtāh* is changed to *šābtāh* = she rested. The Vulgate understands the text on similar lines: "not for a moment has she returned home," and the Peshitta also treats the basic text freely with " . . . even until the rest-period."

**[2:4–5]** Interest now centers on Boaz. How will he react to a foreign woman such as Ruth gleaning in his field? Will he regard it as her natural right or as something he has sole power over? And if it all depends on his will, what counts for more—that Ruth is a foreigner or that she has married into the family?

The meeting between Boaz and the harvesters begins with an exchange of greetings in the form of prayers for Yahweh's blessing. The first sentence that Boaz speaks contains Yahweh's name. Where Naomi limits herself to accepting Ruth's plan and neither blesses her daughter-in-law nor offers her good advice as to how to conduct herself, Boaz gives the impression of taking an interest in and caring for his servants. He at once notices that there is a young woman present who is not usually there.

**[6–7]** Boaz now asks his supervisor who the girl belongs to. The same formulation is used in Gen. 32:18 and 1 Sam. 30:13, where it is also a matter of inferior persons being identified through their master. As for Ruth, the supervisor can say that she is a Moabite woman, and that she is the one who came home from Moab with Naomi. In this way Naomi and Ruth are linked in Boaz's consciousness. Whether or not the narrator thereby wishes to make it clear for Boaz that the girl is foreign and alone, with no other protection than a mother-in-law, is a moot point; certainly, the reader knows already. Only Boaz's response will show whether he too realizes her exposed position, and how he will deal with it. Will he exploit it, or will he take responsibility for protecting her?

The supervisor, unsolicited, tells Boaz what the reader already knows—namely, that Ruth has actually asked permission to glean among the sheaves. Ruth has acted in wise pursuit of her plan. She has not regarded gleaning as her right, but as a favor. We are not told how the supervisor answered her.

The last four words of v. 7 have concerned scholars. Previous attempts to solve the problem by correcting the text or by taking the words to be an addition in the margin[89] have not proved convincing. The most reasonable solution is to retain the text and attempt to interpret it in the context of the narrative. When the

[89]Cf. current commentaries on the proposal for emendation, and D.R.G. Beattie, "A Midrashic Gloss in Ruth 2.7," *ZAW* 89 (1977): 122–24, which regards the words as a gloss. This is disputed by A. Hurwitz, "Ruth 2,7—'A Midrashic Gloss?,'" *ZAW* 95 (1983): 121–23. See also the response to A. Hurwitz in D.R.G. Beattie, "Ruth 2,7 and Midrash," *ZAW* 99 (1987): 422–23.

supervisor mentions that Ruth has only sat down for a moment, the purpose must be to emphasize her work effort. She has been gleaning since she arrived apart from a short break. The fact that he makes a point of mentioning the break can quite simply be explained if she is actually resting when Boaz comes, and that is why Boaz wonders who she is and what she is doing in his field.

The reader is thus given a picture of Ruth as a modest, diligent woman who deserves respect. Here again chapter 2 creates the background essential for chapter 3, where we are meant to keep our first impression of Ruth as an admirable woman.

**[8–9]** If we are right to understand v. 7 as denoting that Ruth is taking a short break, the verse forms a suitable transition to what follows. The break in the work indirectly raises the question, Where is Ruth to continue, here or elsewhere? Boaz anticipates the question by asking her to stay in his field. If she was in the middle of the field at this point, the repeated request not to go to another field and not to leave this place would be less understandable. The break from work, on the other hand, contains the possibility of leaving the field completely.

As a positive possibility in relation to the foreign field Boaz mentions his own girls. Ruth is to stay close to them (the same verb as in 1:14). However, Boaz not only wants to keep Ruth in his field, but also promises to ensure that the harvesters leave her in peace.[90] In addition he gives her permission to drink from the water that the farm hands pour out, without which it is impossible to manage the hard work.

**[10]** Ruth expresses surprise and gratitude by throwing herself to the ground in respect. It astonishes her that a wealthy Israelite should take care of a foreign woman, and the reader is supposed to share this wonder with Ruth. For even though we could point to several places in the Old Testament that stress duty toward the foreigner, it is the narrator's purpose to draw a picture of Boaz as one who does more than could be expected of him.

Ruth's reply is subtle and demonstrates the author's ability to create cohesion in the narrative. We might offhand expect a brief thank-you from Ruth — and that would be the end of the conversation. But that is not how the story proceeds. Instead Ruth poses a question that not only keeps the conversation going but also shows that she regards Boaz as the end of her journey. He is the man whose favor she has been seeking. A further refinement is the wordplay on the likeness between the root *nkr*, which in the Hiphil means "acknowledge," and the word for "foreign," *nokriyyāh*. The author thus links two things that are

---

[90]Presumably there is a fear of sexual attack. The same verb is used in Gen. 20:6, where God in a dream announces to Abimelech that he has protected him from "touching" Sarah.

normally kept apart. Linguistic similarity is used to maintain a connection in content that brings the foreign Ruth closer to Boaz.

**[11–12]** Boaz's reply constitutes the climax of the chapter.[91] It now appears that Ruth is not so unknown to him after all. He has already heard of her. Some scholars use this feature to support the thesis that Boaz has long been interested in Ruth without letting her notice his infatuation. But that is hardly the author's purpose. In any case Boaz is not so interested as to have done anything practical to help the two women whom he knows belong to Elimelech's family. The tension is rather maintained by the question of whether Ruth can make him so interested that she and Naomi can gain a secure future in Bethlehem.

In his reply Boaz notes Ruth's loyalty to her mother-in-law—presumably this must have consequences for his own attitude. Since she has demonstrated loyalty to her husband's family, should he too not take his responsibility for the family, and therefore Ruth, seriously?

The reply is formed so as to create a number of associations in the reader. It is not only Ruth who at one point left her father, mother, and native land to travel to a people she did not know beforehand. A similar journey was undertaken by Abram when he set out on his journey to Israel (Gen. 12:1–3). And it is this story that is called to mind when Boaz reformulates Naomi's wish that Yahweh show goodness to her two daughters-in-law, just as they had shown goodness to their husbands and to her (1:8). Boaz wants the God of Israel to repay Ruth by merit, so that she receives her full reward. In this formulation we hear an echo of the words to Abram in Gen. 15:1: "Fear not, Abram, I am your shield! Your reward will be very great."[92] That the use of "reward" implies the birth of many offspring is clear from what follows. Abram complains about having no son, and in answer receives Yahweh's promise that his offspring shall be as the stars of heaven.

Ruth on the other hand does not complain; instead she prays that she may retain Boaz's favor! When we read this alongside the prayer in Gen. 15:1–5, however, we know what the reward should consist of—and also whom Yahweh has appointed to provide Ruth with the necessary offspring!

The conversation between Ruth and Boaz is extremely subtle. For who is actually supposed to help Ruth? In v. 10 she has spoken of Boaz's goodwill toward her, but when Boaz replies in v. 12 he speaks about Yahweh and hands over the responsibility for Ruth's reward to God. This is seen most clearly in his final words, where he specifies that it is under God's wings that Ruth has

---

[91] Cf. Gow, *Book of Ruth*, 46, who shows how the chapter is chiastically structured with vv. 11–12 as the fulcrum.

[92] See Gow, *Book of Ruth*, 54–55 on the use of the word "reward" in Gen. 15:1; 30:16, 18, where reward is spoken of in terms of offspring. See also Psalm 127:3.

sought shelter. The Hebrew word for wings, *kānāp*, is employed here as a metaphor for God's care, and as such is a well-known image of God as protector (Pss. 17:8; 36:8; 63:8; 91:4).[93]

Boaz's reply is beautifully apposite to the picture of the pious Israelite's expectations of God. What he does not know, however, and what the reader only senses through Ruth's words, is that the protection which Boaz asks of Yahweh he himself is going to provide! Not until Ruth lies beside him at night and asks him to spread the corner of his skirt, *kānāp*, over her (3:9) does the irony of the situation became apparent. For what Ruth asks Boaz to do is the very same fulfillment of what Boaz asked Yahweh to do.

Boaz's wish also links up with that of Naomi for Ruth and Orpah in 1:8, where again the reason given is their goodness to Naomi and her family. In 1:9 the reward is described as comfort in one's husband's house. Perhaps Naomi's wish will be fulfilled, even though Ruth did not comply with her request and return home to Moab.

Boaz's prayer for Ruth occupies a central position in the chapter and can be regarded as a brief summary of the message of the whole book: Whoever seeks shelter under the wings of the God of Israel shall be rewarded.

[13] The further the conversation goes, the more sophisticated its structure appears. Boaz speaks of *Yahweh's* just reward and Ruth responds by repeating the wish that she may win favor with *Boaz,* whom she addresses as "my Lord," just as the Israelites address their God. The conversation advances slowly, and we are made to feel that with each contribution Ruth is one step closer to Boaz. With the patriarchal narratives at the back of our mind we recall Abraham's way of gaining concessions from Yahweh as they discuss the number of righteous people in Sodom (Gen. 18:16–33). Small steps can also take one to the goal.

Where Ruth in v. 10 calls herself "foreign" in relation to Boaz, she now uses the expression "your maidservant."[94] When she further emphasizes that she is of less worth than his own maidservants, she puts his special favor for her into relief.

Boaz's friendly words are taken as "comfort" by Ruth. The verb *niham* (Piel) is often used about God comforting both the individual and the people (e.g. Isa. 12:1; 51:12; 52:9; 66:13; Pss. 71:21; 119:82). To "comfort" in these texts implies a change in the external situation, not just a sudden emotional change. Comfort belongs together with help. If there is any emotional aspect

[93]The expression can be interpreted partly through the picture of the bird that protects its offspring with its wings (Deut. 32:11), and partly through the cherubs who spread their wings above the Ark of the Covenant in the Temple of Solomon (1 Kings 6:23ff; 8:6).

[94]The word *šiphāh* means "maidservant," and according to Sasson, *Ruth,* 53–54, is the designation for the lowest social rank, whereas the word *'āmāh* (3:9) is used of women who could be concubines or wives.

at all, it lies rather in the expression "speak to the heart," though the concept of "heart" does not solely connote emotions but includes will.

It is clear that the scene serves to link Boaz and Ruth more closely. Their conversation is thus often compared with that in Genesis 24 between Rebekah and Abraham's servant, who on behalf of his master is to find a wife for Isaac (see in particular Gen. 24:27 and Ruth 2:20a). But where in the story of Rebekah it is the woman who gives the man water to drink, here it is Boaz who looks after Ruth's needs.

[14] Having already offered Ruth water, Boaz now invites her to eat with the harvesters. Bread was a basic food element in those days. Wine vinegar is a sour wine that quenches the thirst and adds flavor to the bread. The roast grain that Boaz offers Ruth was a special delicacy.

Through the information about food and drink the author shows how Ruth becomes increasingly integrated into the farm community. Boaz is depicted as a generous host who gives Ruth more than she needs. There is a clear contrast with her starting point, when she arrived at the field as an empty-handed foreigner to gather what the harvesters left behind.

[15–16] Boaz's concern for Ruth intensifies after the meal. He gives the farm hands orders to let Ruth glean among the sheaves. This may seem superfluous; according to the supervisor Ruth has already herself asked to glean (2:7). And he appears to have given her permission, since she has been at work for a long time before Boaz arrives. The author's purpose is therefore rather to give Boaz the opportunity not just to formulate his permission but also to make it explicit, so that his favor to Ruth is apparent.

The orders to the farm hands not to harass Ruth are a slightly varied version of v. 9 (see also v. 16 and v. 22). What nuances of meaning the verbs might have carried in those days are lost to us. But the following demand to the farm hands that they can also pull stalks out of the sheaves is a new turn and another sign that in showing favor to Ruth, Boaz far exceeds what might be expected; gleaners have no right to the grain in the sheaves.

[17] The section ends by establishing that Ruth works on until evening. To make the trip home easier she first threshes the grain out of the heads; even so she has gathered about an ephah, corresponding to 29–50 (U.S.) pounds. Jack M. Sasson points out that a comparison of this weight with information from Mari as to the daily ration for a worker in ancient Babylonian times shows that Ruth has gathered enough grain for several weeks' consumption.[95] Of course, the important thing is not to find out exactly the actual weight but to be overwhelmed

---

[95]Sasson, *Ruth*, 57.

by Boaz's generosity to Ruth, a motif that returns at the end of chapter 3, where Ruth is given grain to take home to Naomi after the night at the threshing floor.

The most pressing problem, the lack of food, has now been solved for a while. Boaz has himself fulfilled part of the wish he expressed in v. 12, where he asked Yahweh to reward Ruth for all that she had done. But this is no lasting solution. Ruth is still a childless widow and has no provider.

# Ruth 2:18–23

### Naomi and Ruth discuss what has happened

2:18 She took it and went into town, and her mother-in-law saw what she had gathered. Then she took out what she had saved when she had eaten her fill, and gave it to her. 19 Her mother-in-law asked her, "Where have you been gleaning today, where have you been working? Blessed is the man who acknowledges you!" Then she told her mother-in-law whom she had worked with and said, "The man that I have been working with today is called Boaz." 20 Then Naomi said to her daughter-in-law, "May he be blessed by Yahweh who has not failed in his loyalty to the living and the dead." And Naomi told her, "That man is our relative, he is one of our redeemers." 21 Then the Moabite Ruth said, "He also told me: 'Stay with my farm hands until they are completely finished with my harvest.'" 22 And Naomi said to her daughter-in-law Ruth, "It is good, my daughter, that you go together with his girls, for then no one can harm you in another field." 23 So she kept close to Boaz's girls and gleaned until the barley harvest and the wheat harvest were over; but she lived with her mother-in-law.

[2:18] Ruth's return to Naomi is narrated in a slow progression. First Naomi gets to see the grain that Ruth has gathered in the course of the day. Ruth has more than fulfilled the expectations that Naomi could have had of her. Then the leftovers of the meal are brought out, and it is specified that Ruth gives them to Naomi.

[19–20] The conversation shows that when Naomi sees what the day has yielded for Ruth she realizes something special has happened. In the morning Ruth had spoken of seeking a man who would show her favor. Naomi can now see her success, and therefore needs to know where Ruth has been, while offering her blessing beforehand on the man with whom Ruth has worked. Naomi does not repeat the formulation of the morning, "show favor," but uses instead the expression "acknowledge" about the owner of the field. Her words echo Ruth's to Boaz when she expressed her surprise at being acknowledged as a foreigner (v. 10).

Only now does Ruth reveal where she has been working. Naomi is kept guessing for as long as possible, right up to the last word in the sentence: Boaz. Naomi reacts with another blessing, followed by her interpretation of events. It is not coincidence that Ruth has been working in Boaz's field but a sign of Yahweh's loyalty to Elimelech and their two sons as well as to herself and Ruth. Boaz has acted in keeping with his membership of Elimelech's and his own family. Even though he never mentioned "family" to Ruth, he has acted accordingly.

A similar blessing to Naomi's is given by Abraham's servant when after meeting Rebekah he exclaims in gratitude, "Praised be Yahweh, my master Abraham's God, for not failing in his goodness and loyalty to my master" (Gen. 24:27). Yet again the story of Ruth parallels one of the central patriarchal narratives.

Naomi's ability to see the hand of Yahweh behind the day's events is not due only to Ruth's report and the gift of food. A further factor is added to the account by Boaz being one of *our* relatives. At the end of chapter 1 Naomi was bitter, feeling rejected by God and silent, almost distant, toward Ruth. Now she speaks of Ruth as part of *our* family, and praises Yahweh for his faithfulness. Boaz is no longer only a relative of Elimelech and Naomi (cf. 2:1, 3), now he is Ruth's relative too, as Naomi repeats, through the use of "*our* kinsman-redeemer."[96]

What Naomi more precisely reads into the word "redeemer," *gōʾēl*, is not explained. So far it appears to be a relative of whom she has expectations of assistance. But the lack of clarity at this point fits in with the narrative method so far. Only slowly will it be revealed that perhaps there is a future for Naomi and Ruth in Bethlehem. When Naomi returned from Moab, the main impression was that as a childless widow she was a woman with no future. Then we heard that she had this relative of Elimelech's called Boaz, but we were not told what to expect of him. Now we know he is a redeemer.

Nor is it the author's intention at this point to delineate what Boaz has committed himself to. Many scholars believe that as redeemer he is duty-bound to marry the widow of a close relative, but if this were so, the next step would hardly be the threshing floor, but open dealing at the town gate. Moreover, in Naomi's conversation with her daughters-in-law in chapter 1 it was clear that she did not expect any of Elimelech's family in Bethlehem to offer to marry

---

[96]W. E. Staples, "Notes on Ruth 2:20 and 3:12," *AJSL* 54 (1937): 62–65, has argued for a family having only one redeemer, suggesting that in 2:20 and 3:12 Boaz is *not* the man in question. This requires that the particle *min* (2:20) be read as a negation and *'im* (3:12) likewise. Support has not been forthcoming, since the scene in chap. 4 requires that there are two possible redeemers.

her. If the girls were to have new husbands in Judah, Naomi would have to give birth to them.

In relation to the context and the whole narrative method employed by the author it must therefore be thought unlikely that he uses the word "redeemer" to point to a particular legal safeguard that the women can call upon. The concept of redeemer simply means that the women can expect help from him. What form this might take and how they can acquire it, the reader is not told; but that is the task of the next two chapters (see also the concept of redeemer in the section on pp. 74–75)

Even though Boaz has now been presented in a particularly positive light, we must remember that it was not he who took the initiative to contact his relatives when they returned from Moab. Not until Ruth turns up in his own field does he perform a relative's duty. The following chapter will show how the women still have to take the initiative. The situation is fluid, and Boaz is only one of their redeemers.

**[21–22]** Hardly have we been informed that Boaz is the redeemer before Ruth is spoken of as "the Moabite" again. If Boaz is to act as redeemer for both women, we must not forget that one of them is a foreigner. In such a case he would be performing more than his duty. Ruth now tells Naomi that he has urged her to stay close to the farm hands during the harvest, but in doing so she misquotes Boaz, who in v. 8 told her to stay close to his girls. The Ruth who in 1:14 linked her life to another woman is apparently choosing to stay close to the men.

Ruth's account to Naomi contains two further items of particular importance: she is both to stay in his field and to continue until the harvest is over. Naomi reacts only to the first. Whereas that morning she had allowed Ruth to leave without apparently caring too much about her safety, she now becomes a worried mother-in-law who wants Ruth to stay away from the men, so she makes it clear that Ruth should stay close to Boaz's girls. Her words thereby become an echo of Boaz's request in v. 8. How is it that they agree, these two who never meet?

**[23]** Actual practice follows Boaz's and Naomi's wishes, as the final description makes clear; it is Boaz's girls that Ruth works with during the harvest. In a second item of information the author reminds us that the harvest included both the barley and the wheat harvest,[97] i.e., the period April–May.

---

[97]The harvest period is circumscribed by two festivals, Passover, which falls at the beginning of the barley harvest, and the Festival of Weeks (at Pentecost), which is linked to the wheat harvest. The two festivals are separated by a seven-week interval.

Naomi now knows that Boaz is willing to act as a relative, and she can begin to consider how the future will be formed.

While the narrator's strategy throughout the chapter has been to bring Ruth and Boaz closer and closer together, he ends with a brief remark that Ruth continued to live with her mother-in-law. But for how much longer? asks the reader. As in 1:22 this is a hinge used to join one rounded episode to the next.

# III. RUTH SEEKS OUT BOAZ
# AT THE THRESHING FLOOR

# Ruth 3:1–6

### Ruth accepts Naomi's plan to go to the threshing floor

3:1 Her mother-in-law Naomi said to her, "My daughter, shall I not get you a home where you can be well off? 2 Listen! Boaz, whose girls you were together with, is in fact our relative, and he will be winnowing barley at the threshing floor tonight. 3 Wash and perfume yourself now. Put on your cloak and go down to the threshing floor; but do not reveal yourself to the man before he is finished eating and drinking. 4 Then when he lies down, you must watch to see where he is lying. Then you must go over and uncover yourself at his feet[a] and lie down; then he is sure to tell you what to do." 5 She answered her, "Everything you say I will do." 6 Then she went down to the threshing floor and did everything that her mother-in-law had instructed.

a. This can be translated, "Then you must go over and uncover his feet and lie down." See below.

The chapter consists of three parts: vv. 1–6: the initial conversation between Naomi and Ruth at home, vv. 7–15: the meeting between Ruth and Boaz out at the threshing floor, and vv. 16–18, the closing conversation between Ruth and Naomi at home. There are changes of place as well as of time. The preparations are made before it gets dark, the meeting at the threshing floor takes place under cover of the darkness, and the report to Naomi is made at daybreak. Again this chapter has a chiastic structure, with vv. 10–11 occupying the same central position as vv. 11–12 did in chapter 2. In both places it is Boaz's reply to Ruth that is the fulcrum.[98]

[98]Cf. Gow, *Book of Ruth,* 63–65. Edward F. Campbell, Jr. points out that the use of the signifier serves to link chap. 3 to the previous two and gives as examples the connector between 3:1 and 1:9, between 3:9 and 2:12, between 3:10 and 1:8 and 2:20, between 3:11 and 2:1, and between 3:17 and 1:21. See Campbell, *Ruth,* 130.

**[3:1]** Whereas it was Ruth who was active in chapter 2, it is now Naomi who takes the initiative at the start of chapter 3. Her suggestion that she find a good home for Ruth links up with her blessing on Ruth in 1:9. There the word *mĕnûḥāh* was used to denote the security that Naomi wanted her daughters-in-law to find through marriage; the same wish is now expressed through the word *mānôaḥ*, i.e., a different form of the same root. The reader must therefore assume that subsequent events are to be understood not just as the result of Naomi's planning but also as the fulfillment of her prayer to Yahweh that her daughters-in-law should be happily and securely married.

**[2]** Continuing her marriage plans Naomi points to Boaz, who is their relative. If a young woman is to marry, it is the custom to approach a family member with a view to discussing possible candidates. From chapter 2 we know that Boaz is both a relative and *gō'ēl*, a kinsman-redeemer. But it is unclear whether Naomi imagines that Boaz is to be consulted on the matter or if she has already chosen him as Ruth's future husband. The plan to get Ruth married naturally presupposes that Ruth has no brother-in-law with whom she can enter into a levirate marriage, and that she is free to marry whom she will. *Naomi skips steps in the process.*

**[3–4]** What was still an open question in v. 2 is now answered by Naomi's exhortation to Ruth to get herself ready, visit Boaz at the threshing floor, and lie down at his feet. The only possibility now is that Boaz has been designated as the new husband. It is not Naomi who must visit her relative to discuss Ruth's future, but Ruth alone who is to offer herself as a wife to Boaz.

In the consciousness of the times the threshing floor was linked not only to the practical work that was carried out there but also to the festivities and fertility rites of the harvest celebration (see, e.g., the polemic against the whoring of Israel at the threshing floor in Hos. 9:1).[99] We must therefore consider whether Ruth visits Boaz as part of a religious festival. If so, it recalls the childless Hannah's visit to the holy place in Shiloh, where she prays for a son (1 Sam. 1). Such an intertextual reading of chapter 3 reminds us that a childless woman's visit to a holy place can have a happy outcome.

To fulfill the plan Ruth has to wait for the right moment after the meal; after consuming food and drink at the end of a successful day's work Boaz will be in his most receptive mood. This motif is also known from the network of texts to which Ruth belongs, such as the events at the cave outside Sodom, where Lot's daughters allow themselves to be impregnated by their own father (Gen. 19:30–38) and thus become ancestresses of the Moabites and Ammonites. But whereas Lot's daughters gave their father so much wine to drink

[99]See also Herbert Gordon May, "Ruth's Visit to the High Place at Bethlehem," *JRAS* (1939): 75–78, which argues that the threshing floor served as a holy place.

that they could sleep with him in his ignorance, Naomi assumes that Boaz is himself capable of deciding how the night should be spent. Admittedly Ruth is descended from Lot's eldest daughter, but she does not have to behave like her ancestress down to the last detail.[100]

Even so, it is debatable how free Boaz is to make decisions. The instructions to Ruth to wash and perfume herself are naturally to make her irresistible. This is how the bride prepares herself to meet the bridegroom (cf. Ezek. 16:8–9; Esth. 2:12; Judith 10:3). From the Mesopotamian area there is an account of how the goddess Inanna at her mother's suggestion washes and perfumes herself and dresses up to meet Dumuzi (*ANET,* 639). The purpose of the visit to Boaz is therefore clear enough: Ruth is to get herself a husband.

The reader knows this. Boaz on the other hand does not, and must not know anything until Ruth comes and lies down beside him. The words "lie" and "lay" are keywords in this chapter, emphasizing the sexual overtones of the meeting. Naomi gives Ruth the further instruction to uncover herself at Boaz's feet.

This instruction is not normally translated as above. On the contrary, it is either seen as a prompting to uncover Boaz's feet or as an exhortation to uncover the place beside his feet. In the first case the verb "uncover" has the substantive *margĕlōtāyw* as its object. The word *margĕlōtāyw* is not the usual expression for the feet; but many think that as the object of the verb "uncover" it must be used in the same way as the word "feet," i.e., as a euphemism for the sexual organs (cf. the mention of feet in Isa. 7:20). In the second case the object of the word "uncover" is implicit, and the word *margĕlōtāyw* is a place indication to denote "at Boaz's feet."[101] Some scholars therefore believe that it is Boaz's feet she is to uncover, others that it is the place at his feet.

The old translations have clearly regarded *margĕlōtāyw* as a place indication and rendered the implicit object as the place beside his feet. Thus the LXX has "reveal the (place) at his feet"; the Vulgate translates with "remove the coverlet which hides the place at his feet"; while the Peshitta has "draw near and lie down near his feet," symptomatically omitting the verb "uncover."[102] The Old Latin translation has run into difficulties too, but has chosen a different solution by rendering the sentence as "Ibis et venies et operies te ad pedes eius et dormies," i.e., "Go there and cover yourself at his feet and sleep." In favor of the interpretation of *margĕlōtāyw* as a place indication is first and foremost the fact that *margĕlōtāyw* in v. 8 and v. 14 is clearly used for that purpose. This leads to the object of the verb "uncover" being implicit. What Ruth is

---

[100]The decisive role played by a trick linked to a meal is also known from the traditions of Jacob and Esau, where Jacob first buys the birthright for a dish of lentils and later cheats his father Isaac with the aid of a meal (Gen. 25:29–34; Gen. 27).

[101]For a closer account see Campbell, *Ruth,* 121, and Sasson, *Ruth,* 69–71.

[102]Rabbinical scholars have attempted to interpret the passage to mean that Ruth uncovers her face and not Boaz's feet; cf. Beattie, *Jewish Exegesis,* 72–73.

to uncover at the feet of Boaz is not mentioned directly in the Hebrew text; the reader must draw a conclusion from the context and from other known texts.

The general consensus hitherto has been that the implicit object is either Boaz's feet (possibly understood as his genitals), or the place at his feet. But if we read the portrayal of Ruth's attempt to acquire a husband and children within the intertextuality to which it belongs, there is a further interpretation that gives far better meaning. What Naomi is urging Ruth to do is to go to Boaz, uncover herself at his feet, and lie down.

The verb "uncover" is used in several passages in the Old Testament, but there is no example of a woman uncovering a man. Nearly all the examples have a man as the subject and most often a woman as the object.[103] There are only a few places where men are spoken of as uncovering themselves, and the same is true of women.[104]

What is of interest in the context of Ruth as the subject of a verbal action is therefore any reference to women uncovering themselves; and here it is Isa. 57:8 which comes closest to Ruth. The verb "uncover" is used in Isa. 57:8 without a direct object, but with an implicit "your genitals" (cf. the uncovering of the genitals in Lev. 18:7). The woman turns her back on Yahweh, uncovers herself, and makes the bed wide when she buys the love of the bed from her lovers. A similar interpretation of Ruth 3:4, 7 would mean that it is not Boaz she uncovers, but her own sexual organs.

Jack M. Sasson hints at the possibility of such an interpretation through a comparison with Isa. 47:2, where a woman is uncovered, but he adds that since the verb does not always carry this meaning, we must be wary of "rashly accusing Naomi of urging Ruth on to such acts of boldness."[105]

However, further evidence that the proposed interpretation is the right one comes indirectly from the rendering in the Old Latin translation, according to which Ruth is to cover herself. In this way the meaning is transformed into its logical opposite, and uncovering becomes chaste covering. The old translators have been in no doubt as to what Ruth was to do, but have elected to formulate it via a euphemism. The rabbinical interpretation of the passage points in the same direction, maintaining that it is her face that Ruth is to uncover.

But is this anything other than a possibility? Can it ever be a probability? As we have seen, women are never depicted as uncovering men in the Old Testament. The closest example of a similar action would be Deut. 25:11–12, which condemns a woman who in helping her husband in a fight seizes his opponent's

---

[103]Cf. the legislation in Lev. 18:6ff with the prohibitions against uncovering a close female relative, that is, having intercourse with her.

[104]Regarding men who uncover themselves see Gen. 9:21; Ex. 20:26; 2 Sam. 6:20. Regarding women who uncover themselves see Lev. 20:18; Isa. 57:8; Ezek. 23:18.

[105]Sasson, *Ruth*, 70.

private parts.[106] But neither there nor in Genesis 19, for that matter, is the word "uncover" employed. Thus the author of Ruth would find it difficult to convince his readers that Ruth should begin the meeting by uncovering Boaz. To be fair, the action of women uncovering themselves is rare in the Old Testament, and when it does happen, it is met with clear condemnation.

All scholars agree, however, that Ruth's action is not an ordinary one. Against the suggested interpretation it cannot therefore be claimed that such a decent woman would not behave in this way. For the point of the book is precisely that Ruth, urged on by her mother-in-law, does the extraordinary and is rewarded for it.

A further point in favor of this interpretation of Ruth's unusual action is the close parallel between Ruth and Tamar. (For a discussion of the link between Genesis 38 and the book of Ruth see the Introduction, pp. 13–17.) Several times we have seen how the author makes use of traditions from the patriarchal narratives, one of the most obvious examples being the reproduction of motifs from Genesis 38. Both stories deal with women who have lost their husbands. Tamar indeed has lost two, and must face the fact that she will probably never get the third brother whom she could expect to wed according to the rules of levirate marriage. Common to both Ruth and Tamar is that they are marginalized, and that by a trick rather than the agency of the law they acquire the seed that can make them pregnant and produce the required heir. And the trick is closely linked to their roles as women.

Thus both Tamar and Ruth choose clothes as a code for their sexuality.[107] Tamar puts on the prostitute's veil when she offers herself to her father-in-law. She hides her identity[108] and achieves her goal. Ruth does the opposite. She uncovers her sexual organs and invites Boaz to cover her with the corner of his garment. Ruth reveals her identity to Boaz and thus receives his immediate acceptance of her wish. Each in her own way uses her clothing to signal the same message. But where Tamar only wants Judah's seed so that she can become pregnant, Ruth is looking for a permanent relationship. By depicting her as naked the author emphasizes the purpose of Ruth's visit to the threshing floor: Boaz must cover her, i.e. take her as his wife (see also the commentary on v. 9).

The account thus belongs within the network of stories about women that we find especially in the patriarchal narratives. In a critical situation Ruth chooses to

[106]Cf. also Calum M. Carmichael's surprising explication of the background for this law: the Deuteronomist has read the book of Ruth and has been frightened by what women could get up to when Ruth of all people does such things. And so he hastens to formulate a law! Calum M. Carmichael, "A Ceremonial Crux: Removing a Man's Sandal as a Female Gesture of Contempt," *JBL* 96 (1977): 321–36.

[107]For further discussion of clothing as a code see Nelly Furman, "His Story Versus Her Story: Male Genealogy and Female Strategy in the Jacob Cycle," *Semeia* 46 (1989): 141–49.

[108]The identity of persons is an important theme in Genesis 38, where Tamar hides her true identity behind the veil but receives as Judah's pledge two symbols of his identity: his seal and his staff.

stake everything on the survival of the family—as did her ancestress in the cave outside Sodom; as did one of Boaz's ancestresses, Tamar, on the way to Timna.

[5–6] According to Naomi's instructions Ruth must leave it to Boaz to decide her next move. Ruth accepts Naomi's plan without comment and goes to the threshing floor. But before long the reader realizes that Ruth is not following Naomi's advice to be passive and leave everything to Boaz.

# Ruth 3:7–15

### Boaz again shows favor to Ruth

3:7 When Boaz had finished eating and drinking and was well satisfied, he went over and lay down beside the grain pile. Then she approached him unnoticed, uncovered herself at his feet and lay down. 8 But at midnight he woke up with a start and felt around; then he discovered that it was a woman who lay at his feet. 9 He asked, "Who are you?" She answered, "I am Ruth, your maidservant. Spread the corner of your garment[a] over your maidservant, for you are a kinsman-redeemer." 10 He said, "The Lord bless you, my girl! The loyalty you show now is greater than what you have previously shown. For you do not go after the young men, poor or rich. 11 But do not be afraid, my girl, all that you ask for I will do for you. Everyone at the town gate knows that you are a woman of great character. 12 And it is right, I really[b] am a kinsman-redeemer; but there is a kinsman-redeemer who stands closer than I. 13 Stay here tonight. If in the morning he is willing to redeem you, all right, let him redeem; but if he has no wish to redeem you, then I will redeem you, as surely as Yahweh lives! Lie here until the morning." 14 So she remained lying at his feet[c] until it was morning; but she got up before[c] anyone could be distinguished, for he[d] said that it must not be known that the woman had come down to the threshing floor. 15 Then he said, "Take the shawl you have over you and hold it out." Then she held it out, and he measured six measures of barley into it and put it on her back. Then he[e] went into town.

a. Qere and several manuscripts have the dual form: "your wings."

b. Ruth 3:12 contains uncommonly many particles in the introduction. A number of scholars[109] therefore omit *'im* without altering the meaning of the verse.

---

[109]For example, Gerleman, *Rut*, 30. See also Campbell's deliberations on how the number of particles in the verse can be lessened (Campbell, *Ruth*, 125). In addition see the very unusual exegesis of the passage in Staples, "Notes on Ruth 2:20 and 3:12," *AJSL* 54 (1937): 62–65, interpreting the statement as Boaz's repudiation that he is a kinsman-redeemer.

c. The reading here is qere.

d. The Peshitta renders this in the feminine, so that it is Ruth who guards her reputation. In consequence the verb is corrected to the 1st pers. sing., "I had come," and "the
woman" is omitted. The correction fits in well with the Peshitta's puritanical attitude to
the story.

e. Both the Peshitta and the Vulgate as well as a number of manuscripts render this
in the feminine. This is presumably a correction based on the context, since v. 16 deals
with Ruth's return to the town.

[3:7] Boaz now acts as Ruth had predicted. It is spelled out that the meal
puts him in good humor, and thus some of the preconditions for persuading
him to marry Ruth are already fulfilled. There has been much discussion as to
why Boaz lies down by the grain pile. Is it in order to guard it, as some have
thought, or because certain religious rites have taken place alongside the harvested corn? We simply do not know, but the course of events shows that Boaz
has need of the corn, since he will give Ruth a present to take home.

Ruth then follows Naomi's plan and arrives unnoticed beside the sleeping
Boaz. She uncovers herself, but does not reveal her identity.

[8–9] Boaz awakes suddenly at midnight. The reason is not given, but the
time indicates that it is the hour of destiny.[110] Boaz is not well-rested, but
wakes with a start. The Hebrew verb implies that he is seized with fear and is
shivering. Over the years scholars have given many and various explanations.
Some think that he is shaking from cold because Ruth has uncovered his feet,
others that Ruth has touched him. And the ancient rabbis discussed whether
Boaz awoke because his sexual needs had been aroused. Jack M. Sasson has
suggested that the background for a grown man waking up in fright in the middle of the night is to be found in the fear of the demon, Lilith, about whom it
was said that at night she imposed herself in intercourse with sleeping men,
thereby diminishing their potency. In the Old Testament Lilith is spoken of
only in Isa. 34:14, where she is linked to the desert; and there is no mention of
her sexual aggression. But if Sasson is right, then Boaz is frightened that it is
Lilith who is haunting him.[111]

Fewell and Gunn[112] suggest another possibility, on the assumption that
Ruth has uncovered Boaz. He wakes suddenly at midnight and discovers to his
horror a woman lying with him and his clothes in disarray. He does not know
whether Ruth has exploited the situation and had intercourse with him while
he was asleep. One can never be sure with a Moabite woman (cf. Lot's daughters, Gen. 19:30–38). If that is the case and the relationship has consequences,

110Cf. Ex. 12:29; Judg. 16:3; Job 34:20.
111Sasson, *Ruth,* 75–78.
112Cf. Fewell and Gunn, *Compromising Redemption,* 1990, 86–87.

he is in a nasty predicament that could lead to him being forced to marry a Moabite woman of low social status in a match that no wealthy man of his time would welcome.

Such an interpretation is legitimate, though the text itself offers extremely sparse information. It merely describes Boaz's reaction without stating what he is reacting to, and specifies that by feeling around he discovers there is a woman at his feet. This ought to calm him down, if it was a demon he was worried about. Sasson adds here that the narrator has doubtless been quietly amused at the thought that Ruth should turn out to be as aggressive as Lilith.

When Boaz asks her who she is, he quite correctly employs the 2d pers. fem. pronoun, to which Ruth responds with her name and status as his maidservant, though with no mention of revealing her Moabite origins. In the context the word "Moabite" would create a distance between the two and is therefore avoided. Ruth's use of "your" before maidservant anticipates the course of events. She is not just any old maidservant but already through her work in the field has acquired a certain attachment to Boaz. She further defines Boaz's affiliation to herself by referring to him as kinsman-redeemer and asking him to spread the corner of his garment over her.

The use of the word *kānāp* at this juncture has given rise to various interpretations, since the consonant text (ketib) has the singular—a corner—whereas the vowel text (qere) and several manuscripts have the dual. If we read the vowel text—your wings—Ruth is asking for Boaz's general protection, and it becomes clear that there is a link back to 2:12, where the dual form is used of Yahweh's protective wings.

But it is more correct to retain the consonant text—the corner of your garment—so that the purpose of Ruth's request is that Boaz should marry her.[113] This fits in better with the narrative action and corresponds to the usage in Ezek. 16:8, where Yahweh finds Jerusalem as a naked woman and marries her by spreading the corner of his garment over her.[114] Calum M. Carmichael in a comment on the book of Ruth points out that to spread the corner of one's garment over a naked woman was a symbol of marrying her. But he puts the "naked" in parentheses since in this context he does not believe that Ruth is naked.[115]

Also on the basis of the ketib form it is apparent that the narrator wishes to make the link with 2:12. Boaz's pious wish in 2:12 is now to be fulfilled. But it is Boaz himself who is to take responsibility for the protection he wished for

---

[113]For a closer treatment of this symbolic action see Paul A. Kruger, "The Hem of the Garment in Marriage: The Meaning of the Symbolic Gesture in Ruth 3:9 and Ezek. 16:8," *Journal of Northwest Semitic Languages* 12 (1984): 79–86.

[114]Cf. also the form of the prohibition against intercourse with one's mother in Deut. 23:1, where it is laid down that no son may lift the corner of his father's garment. See also Deut. 27:20.

[115]Calum M. Carmichael, "A Ceremonial Crux: Removing a Man's Sandal as a Female Gesture of Contempt," *JBL* 96 (1977): 332–33.

Ruth by spreading the corner of his garment over her and marrying her. The narrator is here trying to create a connection between Boaz's first meeting with Ruth and this second one.

If we now relate the depiction of Ruth's preparations, washing, perfuming, dressing, to the events at the threshing floor, to the self-exposure, and to the request that she be covered by the corner of Boaz's garment, it becomes clear that the natural understanding of the sequence is that it is Ruth who uncovers herself and not Boaz who is uncovered. The prayer that she be covered is given meaning precisely because she is naked.

The request for marriage is motivated with a reference to Boaz as kinsman-redeemer. But how valid is this justification? Was it really by the laws of the time the duty of a kinsman-redeemer to marry the childless widow, such as Ruth the Moabite?

One of the major problems in the book of Ruth is the exact meaning of the concept of *gō'ēl*, kinsman-redeemer, in this context. Scholars have for the most part taken as their starting point the regulations regarding the duty of kinsmen-redeemers and of levirate marriage. This is due to the fact that chapter 4 speaks not only of the purchase of Naomi's field, but also of the purpose of marriage between Ruth and Boaz as the birth of a son for Mahlon, in order that the deceased husband can retain his name to his property. The purchase of the field belongs with the duties of a kinsman-redeemer, while the creation of a son for a deceased husband is known from the regulations governing levirate marriage (for a closer discussion of levirate marriage see pp. 84–85). The problem is therefore often formulated as the question of the degree to which the marriage between Ruth and Boaz is a levirate marriage, and as such part of Boaz's duty as kinsman-redeemer.

## EXCURSUS on the Duties of the Kinsman-Redeemer

The duty to act as kinsman-redeemer, *gō'ēl*,[116] is mentioned in the Old Testament laws in connection with the sale of property. When an Israelite is forced to sell his land

---

[116]See further in Millar Burrows, "Levirate Marriage in Israel," (1940): 23–33; "The Marriage of Boaz and Ruth," *JBL* 59 (1940): 445–54, and "The Ancient Oriental Background of Hebrew Levirate Marriage," *BASOR* 77 (1940): 2–15; A. R. Johnson, "The Primary Meaning of the Root *g'l*," *VT Supp* 1 (1953): 67–77; Thomas and Dorothy Thompson, "Some Legal Problems in the Book of Ruth," *VT* 18 (1968): 79–99; Robert Gordis, "Love, Marriage, and Business in the Book of Ruth: A Chapter in Hebrew Customary Law," in *A Light unto My Path: Old Testament Studies in Honor of Jacob M. Myers*, ed. Bream, Heim, and Moore, 1974, 241–64; Donald A. Leggett, *The Levirate and Goel Institutions in the Old Testament, with Special Attention to the Book of Ruth,* 1974; Jack M. Sasson, "Ruth III: A Response," *JSOT* 5 (1978): 49–51; Beattie, "Ruth III," and "Redemption in Ruth, and Related Matters," *JSOT* 5 (1978): 39–48, 65–68; Eryl W. Davies, "Inheritance rights and the Hebrew levirate marriage," *VT* 31 (1981): 138–44 and "Ruth IV 5 and the duties of the *gō'ēl*," *VT* 33 (1983): 231–34. See also the available commentaries.

for financial reasons, the closest relative acts as redeemer and buys the land so that it can remain in the family and not be handed over to an alien (Lev. 25:24–34). The duty of the kinsman-redeemer is justified on religious grounds. The land belongs to Yahweh himself, and therefore Israel must not sell it irredeemably; cf. Naboth's refusal to sell his forefathers' vineyard to the king (1 Kings 21:3). The prophet Jeremiah acts as redeemer for his cousin, when the latter sells his field at Anathoth (Jer. 32:7–15). Redemption can also be the solution if an Israelite through poverty is forced to sell himself as a slave to an alien. In such a case a relative can buy him free, or he can redeem himself if he has acquired the financial means to do so (Lev. 25:47–55). In addition the concept is used in connection with the avenging of blood (Deut. 19:6, 12; Num. 35:19ff.; Josh. 20:3ff). More generally it can be used as an image of God's redemption of Israel (Isa. 43:1). In Job 19:26 the redeemer is either God himself or a guardian angel that Job is expecting to help him in his legal case.

On the basis of the legal material in the Old Testament we must conclude that the duty of the kinsman-redeemer is to intervene in the purchase or sale of property, fields, or houses, as well as in the case of a relative forced to sell himself as a slave; but the redeemer does not appear to be duty-bound to marry a childless widow unless he is at the same time the woman's brother-in-law. If the narrator is operating with the legal regulations that we know of, Ruth's request is outside the normal custom.[117] Admittedly she behaves like a new Tamar, but from a legal point of view her situation is not the same. For where Tamar had a well-founded demand that her third brother-in-law should marry her, Ruth has no brother-in-law to refer to. She is therefore appealing to Boaz to give her what no law can, but only his sense of honor and his will to help a relative in need.

We shall return in chapter 4 to the question of whether the marriage can otherwise be termed a levirate marriage. But so much is already clear—it cannot be a levirate marriage on the basis of Old Testament regulations, since Boaz is not Ruth's brother-in-law. Moreover, even though other rules of the time existed than those we know of from the Old Testament, it is still manifest from the entire narrative so far that the writer does not regard Boaz as obliged to marry Ruth. Thus the reader must assume that when Naomi refuses to counsel the possibility that her daughters-in-law might find husbands in Bethlehem, there can be no one in Elimelech's family who is duty-bound to marry Ruth—or Naomi herself.

Nor does Naomi's plan rest on a legal foundation. She does not call Boaz to a meeting with the elders at the town gate and present her case; instead she

---

[117]See also A. R. Johnson, "The Primary Meaning," *VT Supp* 1 (1953): 67–77, who thinks that the duty of the kinsman-redeemer also included such a marriage, inasmuch as the redeemer is bound to safeguard the life of the family. This regard for the family's survival can be seen in 2 Samuel 14, where the woman from Tekoa lays her case before Solomon and convinces him that the avenging of blood would be at variance with the duty to the family in the case of her son.

resorts to a trick by sending the young widow down to the threshing floor to lie beside Boaz at night. Consequently the reader must expect that from Naomi's point of view there are other means to her end than the law.

But what about Ruth, who uses the word *gō'ēl* in this scene? In describing her the writer emphasizes that she is a foreigner. This is not to be understood in the sense that through ignorance she simply gets a word wrong now and then. In chapter 2 we saw that she was well aware of the custom of gleaning in the field. The narrator does not point to the foreigner's lack of insight. On the contrary, Ruth's unexpected interpretation of the kinsman-redeemer's duty is seen rather as an expression of her resourcefulness in a difficult situation. It does not follow existing law, but it interprets the spirit behind the redeemer concept: care for the survival of the family.[118] We could say that Ruth acts more like an Israelite than her new countrymen do!

Here again the pattern from the Tamar story is repeated. Then Judah had to admit that Tamar was more right than he; now Boaz becomes convinced that he cannot summarily dismiss Ruth if he is to take serious care of the family. Ruth here is penetrating deep into Israelite philosophy and extending the duty of the kinsman-redeemer to looking after weaker family members by including the childless widow among them.

[10–11] Boaz submits to an argument that is unexpected and indeed only hinted at. Just as on their first meeting (2:11–12), Boaz now utters a wish and a blessing by which the narrator creates the expectation in the reader that the wish may one day become a reality. Boaz's praise of Ruth's loyalty similarly comments on what happened in the field when he noted all that she had done for her mother-in-law by traveling with her to a foreign country. But there is a more precise formulation: it is Ruth's choice of husband that is praised. Loyalty in this context is presumably to be seen as a sign of her care for her mother-in-law. Ruth is not choosing on the basis of her own interests. Had she done so, the choice according to Boaz would have fallen on a young man, whatever his financial circumstances. But Ruth chooses from within Elimelech's family, thereby showing that she will preserve her solidarity with Naomi.

When the narrator characterizes this latest sign of loyalty as greater than the first, it is in order for the reader to interpret Ruth's action as an expression of unselfishness. The chapter started with Naomi's care for Ruth but Ruth's decision to take matters into her own hand matches her mother-in-law to the full. Thus the scene between Ruth and Boaz is not seen as a rendezvous between two lovers whose only concern is themselves. It is a question of the continued survival of the family—and Ruth's role as part of that family.

---

[118]Cf. Campbell, who strongly emphasizes that it is the Moabite Ruth who combines the redeemer obligation with levirate marriage. Campbell, *Ruth*, 132–37.

Boaz's next response is to consent to do everything that Ruth asks him. We cannot tell whether Boaz is already considering that as *gō'ēl* he ought to redeem Elimelech's property, as is the case in chapter 4. But the common reading of the concept makes this a reasonable assumption. What Ruth is referring to quite clearly, however, is marriage.

Little by little the narrator has built up a network of remarks that have to do with acting on what has been said. First it was Naomi who declared that Boaz would surely tell Ruth what to do. Then Ruth undertakes to do what Naomi has said, and now Boaz promises to do as Ruth says. The remarks mirror each other, but with an ironical overtone. For as the action unrolls, it is revealed that Ruth actually acts otherwise than Naomi had planned. Ruth speaks up and does not wait for Boaz to tell her what he wants. And not even Boaz's remark can be given credence for long. He may be willing to marry Ruth, but unfortunately there is an obstacle in the way.

The narrator's dramatic play with the characters produces a certain unrest in the reader. Why do they not do as they say, or as they are told? Perhaps the narrator is trying to prevent a too rigid interpretation of the action on the basis of human plans, be they Naomi's, Boaz's, or Ruth's.

The small dislocations in the narrative, which will eventually lead to a goal that exceeds the expectations of all three principal figures, make a theological point. Behind events stands a guiding will that acts through the individual characters without identifying with any single human plan.

Boaz's first reason has to do with Ruth's personal qualities. She is a woman of great character, we are told. The expression *'ēšet ḥayîl* is not common, though it appears in Prov. 31:10 to introduce a eulogy to the wife of noble character. Applied to Ruth it has the function of making her a suitable partner for Boaz, who correspondingly is described as a wealthy man, *gibbôr ḥayîl* (2:1). It is nonetheless worth noticing that Boaz is not just satisfied with giving his own appraisal but says that everybody at the town gate thinks likewise. That his first response should be what others think of Ruth might suggest that his regard for the opinions of others plays a decisive role.

In their commentary on Ruth, Fewell and Gunn stress that Boaz is deeply embarrassed by the whole situation. What will the townsfolk think if he marries a non-Israelite? That simply will not do for a man of Boaz's status.[119]

**[12–13]** Only then does Boaz agree that he really is a kinsman-redeemer, thus accepting Ruth's linking of the redeemer's duty with marriage to a childless widow. We saw earlier how Boaz was not legally bound to marry Ruth. What he now declares himself willing to do therefore goes beyond what could be expected. Yet again the emphasis is on the generosity that Boaz has personified

---

[119]Cf. Fewell and Gunn, *Compromising Redemption*, 87–93.

from the start. He is a man who gives more than his duty demands, even though he does not do so off his own back. And as was the case when they first met, the initiative is Ruth's.

Hardly has Boaz promised to fulfill Ruth's wish, however, before a stumbling block appears. The structure of the action at this point bears a close resemblance to that of the patriarchal narratives. The repeated promises to Abram are time and again thwarted by various impediments that threaten to overthrow the plan for salvation. God has barely promised Abram that he will gain the land and become a great people than famine forces him out of the land and the tribal ancestress is received into a foreign harem (Genesis 12). And Sarai has only just acquired a son through Hagar before her solution to the problem is rejected.[120] As narrative technique these obstacles retard the action and increase the tension, but they also have a theological purpose: God acts in spite of the hardships that arise, be they hunger, childlessness or local custom.

The meeting at the threshing floor between Ruth and Boaz must be regarded as the ideal starting point for a marriage. Boaz's acceptance of Ruth's request can only mean that he is willing to marry her. But the mention of another kinsman-redeemer who stands closer to Ruth suspends this outcome for the time being.

In the light of the many obstacle-motifs in the patriarchal narratives it also appears superfluous that later Jewish tradition and various of its interpreters make a great point of stressing that Boaz was a pious and righteous man who naturally did not exploit the young woman who lay beside him.[121] What the individual reader makes of the nighttime events is of course not in the hands of the narrator; but the narrative plot rests on Boaz simultaneously promising to fulfill Ruth's wish yet telling her that for the time being it is impossible to do so. How will the narrator deal with this impasse?

Boaz's dilemma is reflected in his words to Ruth that another redeemer's decision must be respected—but that she should stay with him for the rest of the night. Here the writer uses the same verb as in 1:16, where Ruth vowed that she would live where Naomi lived. Now it is no longer Ruth who will live with Naomi till death do them part but Boaz who wants Ruth to stay with him—at least for the night! The necessity of asking the other redeemer first implies that Ruth may be taken away from Boaz; but the exhortation to Ruth to stay shows that the real purpose of the narrative is to join Ruth and Boaz together.

However, the other kinsman-redeemer represents a genuine hurdle, as can be seen from Boaz's remark that if he is willing to redeem Ruth, then he should

---

[120]The many obstacle-motifs in the patriarchal narratives create a tension as to the outcome of the divine plan for salvation, not least when Yahweh himself places impediments in the way (cf. Gen. 22). In the Exodus accounts we meet the same motif, when Yahweh threatens Moses' life, Exodus 4, or time and again hardens Pharaoh's heart, Exodus 7–11.

[121]Cf. inter alia Tryggve Kronholm, "Portrayal," *ASTI* 12 (1983): 13–54.

do so. On this point Boaz represents the law. If he and Ruth are to marry, the formalities must first be observed. When this has been done, he will redeem her. The statement is underlined with an oath, "as surely as Yahweh lives." Just as Ruth vows in 1:17 that only death will part her from her mother-in-law, so Boaz promises on oath to marry Ruth.

Again the narrator is employing a technique that reflects a previous statement, thereby adding cohesion to the story, as well as further overtones. For what bearing does Boaz's oath have on Ruth's oath? Can they both be fulfilled or must Ruth break hers in marrying Boaz?

[14–15] The following section serves as a transition from the threshing floor to Ruth's return home. Boaz ended the conversation by asking Ruth to remain with him until the morning. This request is the only concrete direction as to "what she shall do" (cf. 3:4). Naomi had predicted that from the start Boaz would take the initiative, but she was wrong. Only gradually does he become the one who initiates the action.

He it is too who ensures that Ruth leaves the threshing floor just as unnoticed as on her arrival. The reason for this will appear in chapter 4, where the plot depends on none of the men at the town gate knowing of Ruth's visit to the threshing floor, let alone Boaz's promise of marriage. The narrator's wish to demonstrate Boaz's care for Ruth's good name is probable in the light of the apparently forthcoming marriage.

Before Ruth is allowed to go, however, he gives her some of the grain from the threshing floor. No unit of measure is mentioned, but the idea must be that she receives as much as she can carry. And again Boaz shows his kindness.

# Ruth 3:16–18

### Naomi and Ruth discuss what has happened

3:16 She went home to her mother-in-law, who asked, "Is that you, my daughter?" And she told her everything that the man had done for her. 17 She said, "He gave me these six measures of barley, because he said, 'You must not come to your mother-in-law empty-handed.'" 18 Then she said, "Stay here, my daughter, until you know the outcome of the matter; for that man will not rest, he will make sure the matter is settled today."

[3:16–18] In the final verses of the chapter it is again the two women who are talking together, with the conversation following more or less the pattern of 2:18ff. Naomi wants to hear what has happened since Ruth left home, so Ruth gives her version of events.

Regarding what has previously been related, there is an amplification in Ruth's summary. She quotes Boaz as saying that she should not come home empty-handed to her mother-in-law. This is new information for the reader, but the purpose is obvious enough. The repetition of Boaz's words serves to include Naomi in events. Just as it was emphasized at the end of chapter 2 that Boaz was redeemer for both of the women, "one of our kinsmen-redeemers," so it transpires now that Boaz's solicitude embraces both Ruth and Naomi.

The phrase "come empty-handed" reminds us of Naomi's words in 1:21, where she described her own situation as like one who is empty-handed, despite Ruth having accompanied her all the way from Moab. This time Ruth really has changed Naomi's situation. For the moment by providing food, later— or so we hope—by providing an heir.

For it is no coincidence that both chapters 2 and 3 end with gifts of grain. The book uses the need for grain, or sustenance, as a leitmotif, and alongside this the need for an heir—two motifs requiring the essential seed.[122] Without the seed both famine and childlessness threaten. The meeting at the threshing floor gives Ruth the promise of marriage, but neither the wedding nor the pregnancy is as yet a reality. On the other hand she has received a gift of grain to bear.

With the scene at the threshing floor Naomi's plan for Ruth has come close to a happy conclusion. What the law has been unable to provide for Ruth in the form of a levirate marriage, she has been promised through the surprise action, the trick—with the addition, be it noted, of Ruth's unexpected interpretation of the redeemer's task. Boaz is not only astonished to find a naked woman at his feet, he has also met his match in the art of interpreting the law. What he is faced with here resembles to a high degree Judah's experience with Tamar.

However, where the author of the Judah/Tamar story separates them immediately after the discovery of the true nature of the case, the intention in Ruth is that the two should be united. The book thus forms a contrast to Genesis 38 and provides a new version of how the relationship between the two main characters should develop. But before Ruth and Boaz can finally come together, it is Boaz's task to ensure that the law be respected. The other redeemer must first be approached, and the scene, set at the threshing floor, must therefore be followed by a new scene, set at the town gate. Naomi's final remark at the end of chapter 3 vouches for Boaz's determination to seek an immediate settlement. The only question is how.

The chapter ends with a conversation between Ruth and Naomi, the last time we hear them speak. The first three chapters have contained a series of dialogues between them, but from now on they will speak no more, directly or indirectly. The final action awaits them.

---

[122]For the motive of "seed" see Hubbard, *Book of Ruth*, 226, and Barbara Green, "The Plot of the Biblical Story of Ruth," *JSOT* 23 (1982): 55–68.

# IV. BOAZ MARRIES RUTH, WHO BECOMES THE ANCESTRESS OF DAVID'S LINE

## Ruth 4:1–12

**Boaz states publicly that he wishes to marry Ruth, and the anonymous kinsman-redeemer withdraws**

4:1 Boaz had gone up to the town gate and had sat down there. Then the kinsman-redeemer of whom Boaz had spoken came past and he said, "Come and sit down, you there!" And he came and sat down. 2 Then he got hold of ten of the town's elders and said, "Come and sit down!" And they sat down. 3 Then he said to the kinsman-redeemer, "That piece of field which belonged to our relative, Elimelech, Naomi wants to sell, now that she has returned home from the land of Moab. 4 So I thought I would tell you that you ought to buy it now in the presence of the people sitting here as well as the elders of our people. If you wish to redeem it, then redeem it; but if you[a] do not wish to redeem it, then tell me so, so that I know; for there is no one else to redeem it except you, and then me after you." He answered, "I will redeem." 5 Then Boaz said, "The day that you buy the field from Naomi, I[b] will buy the Moabite woman, Ruth,[c] the wife of the deceased, in order to restore the name of the deceased to his property." 6 Then the kinsman-redeemer replied, "Then I cannot redeem, for I do not wish to damage my property. You must redeem what I ought to redeem, for I cannot redeem." 7 Now in former times in Israel it was the case in matters of redemption and property transfer that the one party took off his sandal and gave it to the other in order to seal the matter; this was a valid form of attestation in Israel. 8 The kinsman-redeemer said to Boaz, "You buy!" and he took off his sandal. 9 Boaz then said to the elders and all the people, "Today you are witnesses that I am buying from Naomi everything that belonged to Elimelech, and everything that belonged to Chilion and Mahlon. 10 Also the Moabite woman Ruth, Mahlon's wife, I am buying as a wife in order to restore the name of the deceased to his property, and in order that the name of the deceased shall not be expunged from his family or from his town's gate. You are witnesses to this today!"

11 And all the people who were at the gate, and the elders said, "We are witnesses! The Lord grant that this woman who goes into your house may be like Rachel and Leah, the two who built the house of Israel. Show your power in Ephrathah and be namegiver in Bethlehem.[d] 12 May your house be like Perez's house, he whom Tamar bore to Judah, through the children whom the Lord gives you through this woman."

a. The verb is corrected from 3d pers. sing. to 2d pers. sing. on the basis of several manuscripts as well as the versions, BHS.

b. Scholars disagree on whether to read ketib or qere. The LXX and the Peshitta have qere. Both ketib "I buy" and qere "you buy" make sense in the context, but they lead to two different readings of the plot. In the translation above "ketib" is the preferred reading. See also the commentary to v. 5 below.

c. There is general agreement on correcting *ûmē'ēt* in accordance with v. 10 to *gam 'et* (BHS). *gam* functions as a contrasting particle (cf. Amos 4:6; Micah 6:13), and Ruth becomes the object of the verb "to buy," which requires an object. The renderings in Vetus Latina and the Vulgate also favor the correction. As one of the few, Murray D. Gow[123] argues for the retention of the original text, so that the field is to be bought from both Naomi and Ruth.

d. The expression "become a namegiver in Bethlehem" can also be translated as "become renowned in Bethlehem."

[4:1–2] As predicted by Naomi, Boaz now sets to work on the matter. Traffic in and out of the town goes through the town gate, and Boaz can therefore expect that sooner or later the kinsman-redeemer in question will pass by. In the ancient Orient the town gate and the area in front of the gate was the obvious place to gather. Connected to the town gate were a number of gaterooms where there was room for various kinds of transaction, including legal cases that required a settlement. In Deut. 25:5–10, for example, we read of how cases relating to levirate marriage were to be presented to the elders at the town gate. By sitting down at the gate Boaz has chosen an effective way to have the case discussed in the presence of witnesses.

Whereas in chapter 3 Ruth carries out her ruse at nighttime and without witnesses, in chapter 4 Boaz acts in daylight, in public, and within the law. In contrast to the world of women we are now entering the world of men.

The kinsman-redeemer passes the town gate very conveniently and agrees to sit down with Boaz. Boaz does not refer to him by name, but with an impersonal, "You there," which is surprising. For it is not any old person he is addressing, but a well-known family member whose name he must surely know.

---

[123]Murray D. Gow, "*Ruth Quoque*—A Coquette? (Ruth 4:5)," *TB* 41 (1990): 302–11, and Gow, *Book of Ruth*, 162–65.

The author's anonymization of the man must therefore be an expression of indirect condemnation of him as a man who refuses to safeguard the good name of the family for posterity. He deserves to remain nameless.[124]

In order to settle the matter witnesses are needed, in this case ten of the town elders. The number ten is not prescribed anywhere but is used here as a round figure.

[3–4] The framework for a legal case is now in place, and the reader must expect that the case in question deals with Ruth and her possible marriage. At the threshing floor Boaz had promised to act as kinsman-redeemer for Ruth if the other redeemer was unwilling to do so. So it comes as a surprise that Boaz begins by talking about a field that Naomi wants to sell.[125] With some suspense the reader must ask, Where is Boaz's argument leading? We do not really doubt that Ruth and Boaz will be joined together eventually; the question is how. Edward F. Campbell makes this clear when he says, after making the specific point that the real goal of the book is the birth of a child, "The fun, the tension, the pathos, the excitement have been in getting the hearer or reader there!"[126]

The field belongs to Elimelech, who is described by Boaz as a relative, and the kinsman-redeemer is told that Naomi wishes to sell it. We do not know from where Boaz has this information, since he and Naomi have never met in the course of events. But apart from this the situation is simple enough. The many deliberations by scholars as to whether the field had been leased out while Elimelech and Naomi were in Moab, or whether as a widow Naomi is allowed to own the field in question and put it up for sale,[127] are quite superfluous. Nothing in the text suggests that those present have wondered at the situation or questioned it. Naomi is a childless widow who for financial reasons must sell the family property. Such a sale is a matter for the other members of the family, since the closest relative ought to come forward as kinsman-redeemer and redeem the field. The duty to act as kinsman-redeemer is prescribed in Lev. 25:24–34, 47–55, and is also known from a similar case, where the prophet Jeremiah buys his cousin's field (Jer. 32:7ff; cf. also the excursion on the duty of the kinsman-redeemer on pp. 74–75).

All the townsfolk who have gathered know how a close relative should act in such a situation, and are therefore waiting for him to live up to their expectations. Boaz presents the case carefully and convincingly: either the other

---

[124]According to Jewish tradition the man in question was called "Tob" because in 3:13 Boaz says "all right, [let him redeem]." It is this "all right," in Hebrew *tôb*, that is interpreted as the proper name of the kinsman-redeemer.

[125]The verbal form is the perfect tense, but in legal language the perfect is sometimes used about what is actually taking place. Thus Naomi has not yet sold the field, as some scholars suggest. For further comment see Campbell, *Ruth*, 144. See also Gen. 23:11.

[126]Edward F. Campbell, Jr., "The Hebrew Short Story: A Study of Ruth," in Bream, Heim, and Moore, *A Light unto My Path*, 95.

[127]Cf. the exposition in Sasson, *Ruth*, 111–15.

kinsman-redeemer steps forward as the closest relative, or it is Boaz's duty to redeem the field. There are only these two redeemers, and in this order (cf. 3:13). The other redeemer does not hesitate; he declares that he is willing and the matter appears to be settled by and large.

[5–6] With v. 5 we have reached the central verse in the legal affair itself,[128] for it is here that Boaz turns the screw. The sentence is chiastically formed with the author ensuring that the crucial statement "I will buy" comes at the end. What none of those present has so much as guessed at (nor should they have done) is Boaz's plan to marry Ruth and restore the name of Mahlon to his property. Boaz's announcement radically changes the position of the other redeemer, who had believed that he was purchasing a field from a childless widow and did not hesitate to agree to do so. Normally a kinsman-redeemer would have to agree to give back the redeemed property again, if on no other occasion than in connection with the year of the jubilee (Lev. 25:8–10). But Elimelech's heirs are all dead, and nobody expects the aging Naomi to bring any more children into the world who could later claim the right to their forefather's land. So even though the redeemer had perhaps reckoned that he would have to take Naomi into the bargain, it would be a good transaction, a safe investment that could not fail.

So far in the conversation between Boaz and the other redeemer Ruth has not been mentioned with a single word. It is Elimelech and Naomi whose names are summoned up by Boaz. Nor presumably would any of the witnesses have had Ruth in mind, a childless widow of foreign origin, a marginalized figure. In a masterstroke of dramatic irony it is only the reader who has an inkling of what is afoot. But even for the reader it is a twist in the plot that the union is to have the character of a levirate marriage, where the name of the deceased is restored to his property. Ruth has not asked for this, and Boaz himself did not mention anything about producing an heir for the deceased when he promised to act as kinsman-redeemer.

## EXCURSUS on Levirate Marriage[129]

The regulations for levirate marriage are to be found in Deut. 25:5–10. If brothers are living together and one of them dies without leaving a son, the dead man's brother

[128]For discussion of the chiastic structure of 4:1–11b see Gow, *Book of Ruth*, 81.

[129]Cf. David R. Mace, *Hebrew Marriage: A Sociological Study*, 1953; Beattie, "Book of Ruth," *VT* 24 (1974); Burrows, "Levirate Marriage," *JBL* 59 (1940): 23–33; Burrows, "Marriage," *JBL* 59 (1940): 445–54, as well as Burrows, "Ancient Oriental Background," *BASOR* 77 (1940): 2–15; Davies, "Inheritance Rights" and "Ruth IV 5"; Gordis, "Love, Marriage, and Business"; H. H. Rowley, "The Marriage of Ruth," in *The Servant of the Lord and Other Essays on the Old Testament*, 1952; Thompson and Thompson, "Some Legal Problems"; and the available commentaries.

shall undertake a levirate marriage to his widow and the firstborn son of this union shall inherit the dead man's name so that it shall not be expunged in Israel. If the brother-in-law refuses, the woman is to go to the town gate and present the matter to the elders. The elders are then to summon the brother-in-law and urge him to do his duty. If this too is unsuccessful, in front of the elders the dead man's wife is to spit in the face of her brother-in-law, take off his sandal, and declare, "This is what is done to the man who will not build up his brother's family line" (Deut. 25:9). Such a levirate marriage is undertaken by Onan with his sister-in-law Tamar, when his brother Er dies without issue. The fact that Onan fulfills his duty as brother-in-law only formally rather than in reality leads to his death, according to Genesis 38. The right to levirate marriage in this case was regarded as indisputable, as is clear from Judah's as well as the author's acceptance of Tamar's unusual method of acquiring her rights.

Scholars have in general seen chapter 4 as an example of such a levirate marriage, even though there are no brothers living together here but only distant relatives. Against this it must be argued that if the law regarding levirate marriage had been valid in Ruth's case, she would have been able to turn to these relatives right from the start and ask for levirate marriage; but we have seen that this was not the case. Naomi's plea to her daughters-in-law in chapter 1 to seek a marriage partner in Moab instead would also be less convincing if there were good chances for them in Bethlehem.

If we assume that the narrator is not trying to mislead the reader, the conclusion must be that neither Ruth nor Naomi has a legal right to impose marriage on any of Elimelech's relatives. This has consequences for the interpretation of what follows, in which the decision has to be made as to whether the verb "to buy" is to be read as ketib (1st pers.) or qere (2d pers.). There is an old and widespread tradition for the translation: "The day that you buy the field from Naomi, you must also buy the Moabite woman Ruth, the wife of the deceased, so as to restore his name to his property."[130] But if that is so, then Boaz is imposing on a kinsman-redeemer the duty to enter into a marriage where the firstborn son is to be regarded as the son of the deceased, even though the redeemer is not the brother of Mahlon.

Now it may of course be the case that in the author's day there were other regulations governing levirate marriage than those we know from Deut. 25, so that also more distant relatives would be under the obligation to marry Ruth. But if that were so, Boaz would not have been able to surprise the other redeemer to such an extent that he alters his yes to a no. Both he and the witnesses would have known that it was his duty, and he would beforehand have had to take this into consideration. However, as we can see, the other redeemer

---

[130]Cf. D.R.G. Beattie, "Kethibh and Qere in Ruth IV 5," *VT* 21 (1971): 490–94, who breaks with the agreement hitherto and argues for ketib, "I buy." See also Hubbard, *Book of Ruth*, 58–61, who retains qere, "you buy."

really is taken aback, and it must be because of Boaz's revelation of his own plans for marriage rather than a well-known consequence of a property purchase.

We must therefore conclude that Boaz neither can impose such a marriage on the other redeemer, nor does so. On the contrary, he offers to do something himself that he is not legally bound to, but which he has morally committed himself to at the threshing place, when Ruth told him that he was a kinsman-redeemer. This is why the ketib reading is to be preferred: "The day that you buy the field from Naomi, I will buy the Moabite woman, Ruth. . . . "

Then why should Boaz take a roundabout route via the field? If the redeemer is under no obligation to contract a levirate marriage with Ruth, why could the author not simply let Boaz marry Ruth without needing to ask the other redeemer, and without him letting the marriage take place out of regard for the deceased's name and property?

Let us look at the latter question first. Why must it be a form of levirate marriage? In order to answer this we must again turn to the intertextuality to which Ruth belongs. Behind the story of Ruth is the story of Tamar, where levirate marriage is a central theme. Seen in relation to Genesis 38, which deals with the question of how far men can refuse to take on the duty of levirate marriage, Ruth presents the opposite case: a man who is not obliged to undertake levirate marriage offers to do so. Such is the man who is the ancestor of David.

An early incident in the history of David's family is hereby given its commentary and its corrective. True, there have been strong women such as Tamar who placed the family above her own good name and reputation, and women like Ruth who left all to follow her mother-in-law, but there have also been men such as Boaz who looked after the foreign widow, the Moabitess Ruth, and thus ensured that the family property remained within the family.

The author portrays Boaz as a man who commits himself creatively to the common solidarity of the family in which he has been raised. He strengthens it when it becomes necessary; he does more than can be expected. This is the action of a man of honor.

A motif of some weight in Ruth is loyalty to the family. We can say of both the hero and the heroine that they possess this *hesed* to an unusual degree. Their loyalty is put into relief by the fact that neither Orpah nor the closer kinsman-redeemer live up to the loyalty of the two main figures. The doubling of characters, with two sisters-in-law, one of whom follows Naomi, and two kinsmen-redeemers, one of whom does more than the law requires, serves to emphasize the special nature of Ruth and Boaz.

In addition to this comes the author's clear desire to legitimize both the connection between Ruth and Boaz and their son Obed's right to Elimelech's lands. No one should be allowed to suspect David's family of illegal aggrandizement. Perhaps there is also a further point—regarding David's relationship to Uriah's wife, Bathsheba (2 Sam. 11). David appeared not to worry unduly as to whether the woman he wanted was married or not. That, however, was not the case with his great-grandfather Boaz, who made sure that the law was followed before he involved himself with a woman. Part of the author's literary antecedents are the traditions surrounding David's marital and extramarital relations.

The second problem that needs to be dealt with is why Boaz begins by discussing the sale of Naomi's field. Could he not simply have left the field out of the matter altogether, since it was the field that had necessitated his summoning the other redeemer? The answer is that marriage and property are not independent entities. Boaz cannot marry Ruth without sorting out the hereditary rights involved, and if he is to deal as a man of honor, he must summon the other redeemer and discuss the field.

The organization of marriage and the negotiations regarding property and inheritance to the mutual satisfaction of both parties were a matter of honor in the society of the day. The redeemer has the right and the duty to redeem the field. Boaz cannot disregard him on this point without affronting his honor, and he must therefore begin with the field. But how far the redeemer will go in his care for the two widows in the family is also a question of honor. And it is precisely here that Boaz has a problem. After the night at the threshing floor he cannot risk having the other man taking over the role of the ideal redeemer and demonstrating the extra *hesed* that Boaz has decided for himself. It would be unfortunate if the redeemer also offered to take over Ruth as his responsiblity. So Boaz offers him the field without mentioning Ruth or in any other way drawing attention to her. Only when negotiations over the field are concluded can Boaz reveal his plans.

From a psychological point of view the author's depiction of Boaz is therefore logical enough. Boaz lives in a society where care for the widow is a family duty, and where a man's honor depends on how well he lives up to it. Boaz has no wish to quarrel with a close relative over marrying Ruth as a matter of course and taking over responsibility for Naomi and the family property. That would run the risk of splitting the family. For the other kinsman-redeemer actually has the greater obligation to do so, and might very well want to purchase the field even if it included taking on the women for the sake of shame, i.e., for the sake of honor. Boaz simply has to contact him.

We often imagine our opponents in our own image. What Boaz fears most is a noble relative who takes over the part that he has written for himself. And that must also be the reader's worry. For we too know what Boaz has promised, whatever his reservations. From the outside we can see that the portrait of Boaz is coherent and convincing; there is cultural, historical and psychological support for it.

Danna Fewell and David Gunn[131] go further in the attempt to draw a psychologically cohesive picture of Boaz. Thus they stress that although Boaz was attracted to Ruth, the major stumbling block was that she was a Moabite. Marriage with aliens was frowned upon. The fact that Boaz nevertheless chooses to act unconventionally is very much in order to save his own honor. For if the night at the threshing floor has consequences—and, according to Fewell and Gunn, Boaz is in doubt as to how far Ruth exploited him while he was asleep—then it is important to get the law on his side before anyone discovers what has been going on. Boaz therefore chooses to make a virtue of necessity and to enter into a marriage that must be seen as a gesture of some weight toward a relative's Moabite widow.

To bring the matter to a satisfactory conclusion it is important for Boaz to play his cards so as to give the other redeemer the impression that it is only the field that is for sale. Ruth is therefore not mentioned until the second round, when the redeemer has been offered what is right and reasonable. Just as Jacob gained his elder brother's birthright through trickery, so does Boaz employ a certain cunning to acquire the field to which the closer (i.e., "older") redeemer had first claim. Again Boaz answers to his name as "the shrewd one." The fact that in chapter 3 he himself was subjected to Ruth's shrewdness makes neither the situation nor the name any the less subtle. The wise will fool the not so wise and in between we sense the will of God.

The other kinsman-redeemer must withdraw his offer after Boaz announces his marriage plans, since for financial reasons he has no wish to buy a field that will soon be liable to repurchase by Mahlon's legal heir. This reaction of the redeemer is understandable.[132] Both Orpah and the redeemer choose the safer path, but in relation to them Ruth and Boaz perform the extraordinary. The characteristic narrative strategy again depicts the protagonists as exceeding expectations and breaking accepted bounds.

We have previously seen how the book of Ruth can be read as a transformation of central motifs in the patriarchal narratives. A further element in the answer as to why the narrator makes Boaz take a detour via the sale of the field rather than inform his fellow redeemer of his plans to marry Ruth can be found in the patriarchal narratives, where time and again two motifs are woven into each other. The one is the promise of becoming a great people: in other words, the family and its fertility. The other is the promise of gaining ownership of a land: in other words, the people's right to the land.

Also in Ruth the two motifs work together, with the scene at the threshing

---

[131]Fewell and Gunn, *Compromising Redemption,* 86–93.

[132]Jack M. Sasson visualizes the redeemer not only having to redeem the field now, but also being liable to help out again as redeemer if Naomi and the heir that she will acquire through Boaz and Ruth cannot make ends meet later on (Sasson, *Ruth,* 139).

floor concerning the continuation of the family, and the scene at the town gate beginning with the lands of the family and the duty to keep them. For without land the plan to restore the name of the deceased to his property has no meaning. Both the heir and the land are necessary. The two promises intertwine yet again.

The author's inclusion of both themes, field and family, also creates a close connection with the start of the book, demonstrating how consciously the narrative is constructed. In 1:1–5 Naomi loses both her land and her family. Now she has returned and her position is not reestablished until she has regained both an heir and the right to Elimelech's land.[133]

[7–8] The narrative drama is now interrupted by a stage instruction to underline the distance between the time that the author is describing and the audience's own time. In order to follow the course of events the reader must be told that there was a particular custom linked to the closing of an agreement in ancient Israel. The custom of removing a sandal and giving it to the opposite party to seal the agreement is clearly no longer in use,[134] but the audience is to understand that at the time it was legally binding. The purpose is again to underline that with regard to the right to real estate there must be no doubt. Everything followed the course of existing law. Perhaps in the reference to the way things were done in those days we should also recognize a certain reservation in the practice of law in Ruth. The author may be employing traditions that not even he can grasp the full meaning of.

Precisely who gives the sandal to whom is not clear from the narrative. In Ps. 60:10 Yahweh casts his shoe upon Edom as a sign that he has a claim to the land, which may perhaps be used as evidence that property rights could be expressed in some form of gesture involving the owner's footwear.

More important in this context, however, is the author's play on some of the ideas that are linked to the regulations governing levirate marriage as they are known from Deut. 25:5–10. According to these the man who refuses to fulfill his duty as brother-in-law is exposed to the humiliating treatment of his jilted sister-in-law spitting in his face and pulling off his sandal. The symbolic action serves to underline that every bond is now broken between the two who should have been married.

In Ruth the symbolic action is not linked directly to the marriage but to the field purchase; nor is it Ruth who pulls off the redeemer's sandal as a sign that he has given up all legal claims in the case and in consequence all moral claim to Ruth. Nonetheless it is reasonable to see this action too as a sign that the

---

[133]Cf. Erich Zenger, *Das Buch Ruth*, 88.

[134]In Jer. 32:10–15 the redemption is confirmed by signatures and the sealing of a document in the presence of witnesses. How early this custom has been prevalent is not known.

ideas of levirate marriage are somehow part and parcel of the description of the legal practice.

The scene at the town gate has a masterly structure. By including the patriarchal traditions and the laws of the day governing family rights, the author succeeds in creating an exciting course of action in which the reader is in doubt as to the outcome right to the very last. Whereas the purpose of a law is to make a sequence of events predictable, the task of a story is to keep up the tension. This is why the interpretation of 4:1–12 must take as its starting point the narrative sequence, the book's plot, rather than legal matter, as has so often been the case.[135]

By establishing this wholly unusual situation the author can also increase our uncertainty as to how the case will be settled. Naomi is not just a childless widow; she is also past her childbearing age and has no brothers-in-law. In her case levirate marriage makes no sense. On the other hand, she has a field that the family is duty-bound to redeem, and she has a childless daughter-in-law who has no brothers-in-law either. No law in the Old Testament governs such a dilemma, and thus the outcome is far from predictable, the story doubly exciting. And we can say it is equally successful, for it fulfills the classic demands of being coherent, intelligible, credible, and self-sufficient.[136]

**[9–10]** Boaz's subsequent speech confirms that the agreement has been attested by eyewitnesses, and that he has not only bought the field but also everything else that belonged to Elimelech and his two sons, Chilion and Mahlon. These two are named in reverse order from 1:2, making it impossible to decide from the order which of them is the elder. In the light of the well-known theme from the patriarchal narratives of the younger brother being preferred to the elder, it is nevertheless reasonable to assume that the author mentions Mahlon last in chapter 4 because he wishes to present him as the blessed younger brother who, despite his premature death, survives through his son Obed. Correspondingly Ruth, who is presumably the younger of the two sisters-in-law, is the one preferred and the one whose family lives on.

In addition to the family property Boaz also buys Mahlon's widow,[137] who is again referred to as the Moabite widow to emphasize that the marriage is being undertaken for the sake of the deceased Mahlon. Boaz's nobility is pointed up in the speech; this is how a true redeemer acts! But the meticulous listing of the content of the settlement still cannot hide the fact that Boaz is taking over certain assets to which the other redeemer had a greater right. And these assets

---

135Cf. Nielsen, "Le choix," *VT* 35 (1985): 201–12.

136Cf. Gow, *Book of Ruth*, 144–45.

137In contrast to 4:5 it is quite clear here that Ruth is purchased along with the field. The field is not bought from Naomi or Ruth. The textual correction to 4:5 is therefore based on this point. Regarding the use of the verb "to buy" in relation to marriage see also Hubbard, *Book of Ruth*, 243–44.

amount to more than just a field and a Moabite widow; they include everything that belongs to Elimelech's family too.

**[11–12]** The witnesses confirm the agreement and have thereby fulfilled their real purpose. Just as we sense in Boaz's speech that regard for the deceased Mahlon soon slips into the background, so it does again when the witnesses make their contribution by expressing their best wishes for the bride and groom. Simon B. Parker[138] has argued that there is a connection between this scene and the wishes expressed in a Ugaritic text describing King Keret's wedding. This would suggest that the wedding between Boaz and Ruth is of greater significance than an ordinary peasant wedding.

The wedding wishes are linked in content to one of the basic themes of the patriarchal narratives: infertility. The hopes for Boaz and Ruth are all to do with there being no lack of fertility in the marriage.[139] Admittedly the text can also be understood to apply to Boaz's wealth and power. The expression *waʿāśēh-ḥayîl* can very well mean to create economic wealth; but since it can also be interpreted to mean putting children into the world, the context speaks rather for this meaning (cf. Prov. 31:3; Joel 2:22).

What the townsfolk wish for Boaz is that he be able to father the child that is the purpose of the marriage—and not just one child either. Alongside this comes the wish that he may pass on his name (cf. Gen. 26:18; Ps. 147:4). The two in fact belong logically together.

The well-wishers' desire for Boaz to prove his potency may well be seen as a comment on his relatively old age, with the reference to Judah and Tamar and their offspring pointing in the same direction. Judah was an old man when he became a father, but his virility and fertility were demonstrated by Tamar bearing him twins. The wish is therefore not only that Ruth be as fertile as Rachel and Leah, but that Boaz be as virile as his forefather Judah.

The reference back to the patriarch Jacob's two wives, with the favorite named first, links the marriage of Boaz and Ruth to the establishment of the twelve tribes of Israel. Jacob is also referred to as Israel. May Ruth be a similar ancestress of Israel! Thus it is the creation of a family that is referred to in the comparison between the house of Perez and the house of Boaz. The choice of "house" may also be associated with Nathan's promise, the point being that it is not David who will build Yahweh a house but Yahweh who will build a house for David (2 Sam. 7:11). Again we sense that it is no ordinary couple who are about to wed, but the ancestors of Israel's greatest king.

---

[138]Simon B. Parker, "The Marriage Blessing in Israelite and Ugaritic Literature," *JBL* 95 (1976): 23–30.

[139]Cf. this interpretation of the wedding wishes in C. J. Labuschagne, "The Crux in Ruth 4, 11," *ZAW* 79 (1967): 364–67.

Rachel, Leah, and Tamar represent typical female destinies: the infertile but beloved Rachel; the fertile but unwanted Leah; and the deceived Tamar, who had to secure her rights herself before she could become pregnant. Common to all three is their task as ancestress. While Leah and Rachel built the house of Israel, Tamar became the ancestress of the Davidic royal house.

The mention of Leah in the wedding wishes may refer to the tradition of how it came about that Jacob married Leah in the first place. For just as Judah and Boaz were both victims of a "bed trick" by Tamar and Ruth respectively, so was Jacob a victim of Laban's trick when he discovered too late that it was Leah and not Rachel with whom he had spent his wedding night.[140] When the witnesses offer their wish that Ruth may be like these ancestresses they do not know the degree to which she already resembles them. Boaz, on the other hand, does—and so do the readers.

# Ruth 4:13–17

### The women of Bethlehem rejoice
### at the birth of Naomi's grandchild

4:13 Boaz now took Ruth, and she became his wife, and he went in to her. Yahweh let her conceive, and she gave birth to a son. 14 Then the women said to Naomi, "Praised be the Lord, who does not leave you without a kinsman-redeemer today! He shall become famous in Israel. 15 He shall keep you alive and look after you in your old age. Your daughter-in-law, who loves you, has given birth to him. She is worth more to you than seven sons." 16 And Naomi took the boy and put him in her arms, and she cared for him like a mother. 17 The neighboring women gave him a name and said, "Naomi has had a son!" And they called him Obed. He became the father of Jesse, who became the father of David.

[**4:13**] The marriage is now celebrated and Yahweh gives Ruth the son that was its purpose. In a few words a course of events is described that is in clear contrast with the many childless years in Moab. Behind the happy outcome of the story stands Yahweh himself. He it is who gives Ruth the longed-for pregnancy (cf. Gen. 30:1–2, where Rachel complains to Jacob over her childlessness, but Jacob maintains that Yahweh is in control).

---

[140]See also James Black, "Ruth in the Dark: Folktale, Law and Creative Ambiguity in the Old Testament," *Literature and Theology* 5 (1991): 20–35, with its treatment of the motif of the "bride-in-the-dark" and its appearance in Ruth, in Genesis 19 (Lot's daughters), in Genesis 29 (Jacob, Leah, and Rachel), and in Genesis 38 (Tamar and Judah).

That the child should be a gift from Yahweh is the logical result of a continuity maintained throughout the book whereby both Yahweh (1:6) and Boaz and Ruth (2:18; 3:15) appear as givers of food. The newborn child must also be seen as the fulfillment of Naomi's desire for her daughters-in-law in 1:8–9 and Boaz's wish for Ruth in 2:12. Now Yahweh recompenses Ruth in full for her faithfulness.

In chapter 1 Ruth promised her mother-in-law to accompany her to her native land and people, but not until she has given birth to Obed is she fully a part of the Israelite people. When Lot's elder daughter gave birth to her son, Moab, a part of Israel was split off into a foreign people; now the division is healed in the reunited family of David.

**[14–15]** The women's reaction to the birth of a son is closely related to the central statements in chapters 2 and 3 (2:12 and 3:10). Yahweh receives the praise he deserves in recognition of his beneficence in granting the well-wishers their prayer for Ruth. At first glance it seems surprising that they congratulate not Ruth but Naomi, who through the newborn baby has acquired a kinsman-redeemer. But by allowing the women to address Naomi the author can yet again underline the importance of the family line and Ruth's loyalty to her husband's family. The word "kinsman-redeemer" denotes in the context someone who can provide for Naomi in her old age and is thus used in its broadest sense. As Boaz became Ruth's redeemer, so does Naomi now gain her redeemer.

The role of the women at the conclusion of the book links up with chapter 1. Where Naomi once complained on her return to Bethlehem of her empty-handedness and Yahweh's harshness, the women now celebrate Yahweh's blessing on her in giving her a son. What the women have to say about Ruth, apart from noting that she is the mother of the child, is similarly related to Naomi in that they praise Ruth's love for her mother-in-law. This love makes Ruth worth more than seven sons—a fairly powerful statement when we recall how important it was to have many sons. The number 7 is a round figure that is also used in 1 Sam. 2:5, where in gratitude to God for her newborn son the once childless Hannah praises the God who can help an infertile woman to bear seven sons.

The close relationship between Ruth and Naomi is one of the most important ongoing themes that has held the book together from first to last. Everything that Ruth has done has been stamped with loyalty to Elimelech's family and with her love for Naomi. In one sense Ruth takes Naomi's place when she marries Boaz to perpetuate Elimelech's family. What the aging widow was unable to do for her deceased husband the young, still fertile, Ruth can achieve. The child is therefore not so much Ruth's as the family's, represented here by Naomi.

As well as functioning as a red thread in the book, the mention of Ruth's value for Naomi connects up with a similar statement in the birth legend in 1 Sam. 1. Here it is Hannah's husband, Elkanah, who describes his love for her as worth more than ten sons (1 Sam. 1:9). Hannah does not quite share this opinion, since she immediately goes into the Temple and prays for a son. When read in this canonical context the women's exclamation places Elkanah's self-evaluation in relief. For as will soon be revealed, it is from Ruth that Israel's hero-kings will descend. Her unusual value for Israel is not a result just of her loyalty and her love; it also consists in her being the mother of David's grandfather, the one the women say shall be known in the whole of Israel.

[16–17] Naomi takes the newborn baby in her arms and cares for him like a mother. According to Gillis Gerleman, who understands Naomi's action as a counterpart to the father's recognition of the child, the author's purpose here is to ensure for Obed a genuinely Judaic mother.[141] The child is so closely united with Naomi that the neighboring women exclaim at the namegiving,[142] "Naomi has had a son!" (4:17).

Many scholars believe that the text of v. 17 is incorrect, since there is no direct link between the name Obed and the words about Naomi's son.[143] One attempt to draw a connection, however, is found in the *Targum to Ruth,* where the name Obed, which means "he who serves," is interpreted in relation to Obed's task of looking after Naomi. Another possibility is that the author has no desire to create an etymology but wishes primarily to present the boy as both Naomi's son and the ancestor of David. This happens in the form of two parallel statements, each of which is begun with the mention of the namegiving, but only in the second statement is the name itself given, followed logically by the brief genealogy.

Even though the book of Ruth is a story concerning the election of a woman, the men are also given prominence toward the end. For the purpose of a birth legend is not only to draw attention to the mother but also to the son who is born and who will assume a special role in the history of Israel. In Genesis 38 we hear how Judah acquires two new sons, of whom Perez promises to be someone quite special. In Ruth we hear through the genealogy how Boaz, who took it upon himself to restore the seed of Mahlon, became the father of Obed, who in turn became the grandfather of David.[144] Although both Judah and Boaz are subjected to a ruse before they contribute to securing the family's fu-

---

[141]See Gerleman, *Rut,* 37–38.

[142]In Gen. 38:29–30 it is the midwife who names the newborn child; normally, however, it is the parents themselves.

[143]For instance, some replace the word "name" in v. 17 with a constructed name that would fit the context "son of Naomi." See Sasson, *Ruth,* 175–76.

[144]The thematic link between the stories of Tamar and Ruth has led Donald B. Redford to

ture, in the final genealogy it is they and their sons, and not the women, who are remembered. (See however Matt. 1:1–16.)

# Ruth 4:18–22

### Ten generations are born in Israel

**4:18** This is Perez's family: Perez fathered Hezron, **19** Hezron fathered Ram, Ram fathered Amminadab, **20** Amminadab fathered Nahshon, Nahshon fathered Salma, **21** Salma[a] fathered Boaz, Boaz fathered Obed, **22** Obed fathered Jesse, and Jesse fathered David.

a. The text has the name Salmon; many manuscripts, however, have Salma, which must be correct, given the previous verse. The text is corrected in line with BHS. Cf. also 1 Chron. 2:11, 51, which spells the name Salma differently from Ruth 4:20. Some scholars see this as an attempt to mediate between Ruth 4:20 and 4:21.[145]

[**4:18–22**] The closing genealogy is not concerned with the Moabite Ruth but with Boaz and his family. The genealogy is called Perez's *tôlĕdôt*. The word *tôlĕdôt* is well-known from Genesis 1–11, where the Priestly editor can link the individual narratives through the help of genealogies (Gen. 5:1; 6:9; 10:1; 10:32; 11:10; 11:27), but it is also used in Gen. 2:4, where the creation sequence is described as the *tôlĕdôt* of heaven and earth.[146]

The word *tôlĕdôt* contains the sense of multiplying. And just as the genealogies in Genesis 1–11 must be understood as the fulfillment of God's blessing of man and woman (Gen. 1:28), so can Perez's genealogy be seen as the fulfillment of the well-wishers' blessing at the wedding of Boaz and Ruth (4:11–12).

The genealogy contains ten names, of which only five—Perez, Boaz, Obed, David, and Jesse—also appear in the actual story. There is thus a certain conjunction

raise the following question: "Could it be that we have in both stories remnants of a cycle of legends dealing with David's descent, the main purpose of which was to show how, although time and again apparently on the verge of dying out, the Judaic line which was to produce the great king survived?" Donald B. Redford, *A Study of the Biblical Story of Joseph* (Genesis 37–50), 1970, 17.

[145]This is René Vuilleumier's reading of the context in "Stellung und Bedeutung des Buches Ruth im alttestamentlichen Kanon," *TZ* 44 (1988): 193–210, with the conclusion that the genealogy in Ruth 4:18–22 is older than the version in 1 Chronicles. See in particular p. 195.

[146]For the concept *tôlĕdôt* see Claus Westermann, who among other things stresses that genealogies are of crucial importance in nomadic communities. He therefore regards the genealogy as "eine sehr alte und hochbedeutsame eigenständige Gattung," and not a remnant of individual narratives. Claus Westermann, *Genesis, BKAT* 1, Genesis 1–11, 1974, 9.

between those whose names appear in the story, but the genealogy cannot be constructed on the basis of the story alone. It is therefore probable that the author is using an available Perez genealogy and suiting it to his particular purpose: the prominence of Boaz and David. In that case the genealogy is the starting point for the story (see also the Introduction, p. 27).

This interpretation, however, conflicts with the traditional view, which sees the genealogy as a later addition.[147] An important argument in favor of the genealogy's secondary character is that its content does not correspond to what one would expect from the story. According to this we would expect to see Mahlon's genealogy, since the purpose of the marriage was to restore his name. Instead we get Boaz's genealogy and even in the form of his forefather Perez's *tôlĕdôt*. The fact that the newborn Obed is known as Naomi's son in the story naturally does not make the link between the genealogy and the story any the less problematic.

Most scholars therefore accept one or other variation of the thesis that a later redactor has added vv. 18–22 in order to elaborate the family relationships. The ultimate consequence of this thesis can be found in Otto Eissfeldt's claim that originally Ruth had no connection whatsoever with David's family, but due to the mention of Perez in 4:12 and the name Bethlehem it became at some point connected with the family of David.[148] But is this really a consequence?

Where the genealogy speaks of Boaz as father of Obed, the story stresses that Ruth's son will restore Mahlon's name for posterity. If we compare this with the way Perez is spoken of, it turns out that Perez, in Ruth, is referred to as the one Tamar bore to Judah, i.e., as the son of his biological father and not as the son of Tamar's deceased husband. It is the same case as in Gen. 46:12, where Perez and Zerah are mentioned in the same breath as Judah's first three sons. Again in 1 Chron. 2:3–4 Perez and Zerah are regarded as sons of Judah, in that a distinction is drawn between the three eldest, whom the Canaanite Batshua gave birth to, and the two youngest, whose mother was Tamar. Thus Perez is regarded as Judah's son in spite of the fact that he and his twin brother Zerah should, on the levirate principle, restore the name of Er, the deceased husband.

Admittedly the Old Testament contains only these two stories of childless widows who set out to create offspring for their deceased husbands, but in

---

[147]Cf. the available commentaries on Ruth, e.g. Campbell, *Ruth*, 172–73; Gerleman, *Rut*, 38; Hugo Gressmann, *Die Anfänge Israels (Von 2. Mose bis Richter und Ruth)*, 1922, 268; John Gray, *Joshua, Judges and Ruth*, 1967, 404–5, 424; Max Haller, *Die fünf Megilloth*, 1940, 19–20; Hans Wilhelm Hertzberg, *Die Bücher Josua, Richter, Ruth*, 1953, 281; Wilhelm Rudolph, *Das Buch Ruth, Das Hohe Lied, Die Klagelieder*, 1962, 71–72; Würthwein, *Die fünf Megilloth*, 2–3, 24; Zenger, *Das Buch Ruth*, 10–11.

[148]Cf. Otto Eissfeldt, *The Old Testament: An Introduction*, New York, 1965, 479–80, and Zenger, *Das Buch Ruth*, 11–14.

both cases the genealogy attributes the child to the biological father.[149] The mention of Obed as Boaz's son is therefore not a strong argument for discounting the link between the story and the genealogy in Ruth. On the other hand, the material is too flimsy for us to be able to draw positive conclusions as to the regulations of the time for the assigning of family relationships in such cases.[150]

We can see from the good wishes and blessings in 4:11–12 that the author has not had Obed's genealogy (4:17) as his point of departure, nor has he regarded it as an adequate ending for the story. Boaz is blessed with the wish that his house may be like Perez's house. If the author had been completely free, it would have been reasonable to speak of the house of Israel as a parallel to the mention of Rachel and Leah, or to mention the house of Judah. The best explanation for the author's choosing the not particularly famous Perez is that it was Perez's genealogy that was the basis of the story.

Through a series of structural examinations Jack M. Sasson has demonstrated that the genealogies prefer to put important persons in particular places in the family order: the places in question are number 7 and number 10. In Perez's genealogy Boaz appears as number 7 and David as number 10. We must therefore imagine that the author has arranged his material with this in mind in order to give prominence to two people: Boaz and King David.[151]

Such a practice presupposes a certain authorial freedom over the material. Who could prevent the writer or a later redactor from beginning with another ancestor if it suited the purpose of his story better? Sasson does not answer this, but assumes that to put Boaz and David in the right place the author has had to cut the genealogy at the start. And thus Perez is mentioned first. But is it so clear that the author needed to cut from the top?

Hezron, Ram, Amminadab, Nahshon, and Salma have no function in the story of Ruth, but they appear in the genealogy to ensure that there are ten generations. If the author had been completely free he could have omitted two of them, for example Ram and Salma, who are known only from this mention and the genealogy in 1 Chr. 2. Instead he could have drawn David's genealogy back to Jacob, so that both Jacob and Judah were mentioned. The fact that the author does not do this must be because he was not free to do so. There is much that speaks in favor of the genealogy existing as Perez's own genealogy, probably in connection with the Tamar-Judah traditions. If the author has had to make changes in order to put Boaz at number 7 and David at number

---

[149]See also Campbell, *Ruth*, 172, who thinks that a child born into a levirate marriage such as Boaz's with Ruth may well have been ascribed to both its legal and its biological father.

[150]In general we should be extremely careful about drawing conclusions of a legal nature from a text such as Ruth. Cf. Nielsen, "Le choix," *VT* 35 (1985): 201–12.

[151]See Sasson, *Ruth*, 184.

10, then it must have happened somewhere else in the genealogy than at the start.[152]

Nevertheless, many scholars see it as a problem that the value of a name such as Perez as a signifier cannot be unreservedly positive. Why use *his* genealogy? There is no attempt in Genesis to hide the fact that Perez came into the world as the result of an incestuous relationship between his mother and his grandfather, with Judah serving as the negative background for the praising of the chaste Joseph in Potiphar's house. In this context it is no surprise that Genesis 38 ends with the birth of twins and thus the recognition of Tamar's resourcefulness in a difficult situation, but not with Perez's genealogy. For if the redactors of the patriarchal narratives see Tamar's relationship to Judah as incestuous, in line with that of Lot and his daughters (Gen. 19:29–38), it would be understandable that they had no wish to link David too closely to Judah and Tamar.

The author of Ruth, on the other hand, retains the connection between David and Tamar. By linking Tamar to two other major female figures of the past, Leah and Rachel, he successfully emphasizes the positive features in the tradition of the inventive ancestresses who in a catastrophic situation save the family from extinction (see the Introduction, pp. 12–17, for the positive features of the women's stories). The fact that David is the chosen one can be seen precisely from the women who are found in his family. What others regard with disapproval becomes a sign of Yahweh's election in Ruth. This feature we find repeated in Matt. 1:1–16, where Jesus, the son of David, counts among his foremothers such names as Tamar, Rahab, Ruth, and the wife of Uriah.[153]

By combining a birth legend with a genealogy the author also demonstrates that the election that the birth legend serves to legitimize includes the entire family of David and not just the newborn Obed. In narrative technique the book of Ruth follows a natural course from the lack of offspring to the birth of the wished-for child, who himself becomes an ancestor. The lack of fertility (1:1–5) is replaced by the genealogical documentation of the opposite.[154] And here a long genealogy is much to be preferred to a brief listing of Obed as father of Jesse who was father of David. The blessing of the neighboring women speaks of the house of Perez and its fertility, but it is in vv. 18–22 that the good wishes become flesh and blood.

The author of Ruth has probably drawn on an available Perez genealogy

---

[152]The genealogy is also far too short to cover the period from Perez down to David. Cf. Campbell, *Ruth,* 173.

[153]See also Marshall D. Johnson, *Purpose.*

[154]A general comparison of Ruth with the patriarchal narratives shows that Gen. 11:27–32 is the introductory genealogy that through a conscious expansion of the genealogical form makes infertility a theme, whereas Genesis 49, where Jacob predicts the fate of the tribes (his sons), functions as a prediction of fertility to these tribal ancestors.

alongside the well-known traditions of Tamar and Judah. From this has been created a coherent story that ends with the genealogy of 4:18–22. By reemploying Perez's genealogy and time and again including themes from the patriarchal narratives, the author has told the story of the election of Ruth—and thus of the family of David—in such a way that the story of Ruth becomes a reinterpretation of how God in his time once elected the patriarchs. Through this the author makes his defense of David's claim to the monarchy. Just as the book begins with Elimelech, "God is king," so it ends with David, God's chosen king.

The significant position of the genealogy in Ruth suggests that the author has been writing in a given political situation where David's origins were under discussion and where there was a need for a defense of his family. It is nonetheless extremely difficult to date the book precisely, since supporters and opponents of David's family fought for the right to the monarchy on a number of occasions. There were thus several situations in which David's mixed origins may have been used to refute his right to the throne. We have outlined above (see the Introduction, pp. 25–26) the role that Ruth may have played in the light of the traditions of Jeroboam and Rehoboam. The conflicts between these two pretenders to the throne are among the best-documented, and thus they give a good impression of how power struggles can develop in the Old Testament.

Since the Old Testament is our only source for the early monarchy and the accounts are not written down until long after the period they describe, it is difficult to be certain about what actually happened at the division of the kingdom. What we nevertheless can express an opinion on is the interpretation of Ruth when read in the intertextuality created by 1 Kings. In this context the strength of the book is that it maintains the connection from David's family to Moab (through Ruth) and to Judah and Tamar (through Boaz), but gives a positive reinterpretation of this by demonstrating how Yahweh stands behind the election of precisely this family.

The book of Ruth quite clearly does not have the ideology of David as its point of departure. On the other hand, it is a contribution to the glorification of David to which large parts of the Old Testament testify in their depiction of David as God's elected. But Ruth tells us more than the other texts about David when it places before us the foreign woman whom God elects and blesses.

# INDEX OF SCRIPTURE AND
# OTHER ANCIENT SOURCES

# INDEX OF SUBJECTS

CPSIA information can be obtained
at www.ICGtesting.com
Printed in the USA
LVOW10s2332191216

518021LV00005B/208/P